The Lost Outlines
of J.W. McGarvey

edited by Brandon Renfroe

Gospel Advocate Company
Nashville, Tennessee

Photos courtesy of Lexington Theological Seminary.

Published by Gospel Advocate Co.
1006 Elm Hill Pike, Nashville, TN 37210
www.gospeladvocate.com

ISBN 10: 0-89225-594-3
ISBN 13: 978-0-89225-594-8

"I adopted at the beginning of my ministry a systematic preparation of sermons, by studying the subject carefully till it took shape in my mind, and then by making brief notes of its divisions and subdivisions which I committed to memory. But I left these written notes at home when I started to church to preach the sermon. These skeletons, each of which filled a single page of note paper, I preserved till they were burned in the fire that destroyed my home in 1887."

–W.C. Morro, *Brother McGarvey*

Table of Contents

The Lost Outlines
by Brandon Renfroe

❝**I** have no partiality for volumes of sermons; for I have derived from them comparatively little benefit.❞

Thus wrote J.W. McGarvey in penning what must rank among the most curious opening sentences of any book of sermons ever produced. In 1893, the 64-year-old evangelist spent the summer in Louisville, Ky., occupying the pulpit of the Broadway Christian Church. [1] A stenographer was employed during McGarvey's brief stay, and some two dozen samples of the great scholar's sermons were transcribed. Confident in McGarvey's abilities, the Guide Publishing Company arranged for the publication of his lessons before they were actually delivered.

Motivation of the Volume

The apparent skepticism of McGarvey as to the value of such works seems to stem from an incident earlier in his ministry. After hearing famed pioneer preacher Walter Scott, McGarvey attempted to duplicate the lesson for his home congregation. "It was the first and only time that I have ever deliberately preached another man's sermon," he later wrote, and he compared the experience to "Saul's armor on the shoulders of David." [2] Perhaps that explains why, in offering up his collection of sermons, he cautioned young preachers to "study them without imitating them."[3]

Given his distaste for the genre, why did McGarvey consent to publication? Several factors, occurring in tandem, should be considered. In the first place, McGarvey was practical. In an era when transportation was rather limited, he realized that many who desired to hear him were otherwise unable. He concedes as much in the preface to *Sermons Delivered in Louisville, Kentucky*, stating that they "should certainly prove useful to religious persons who are frequently denied the privilege of hearing the living preacher." If hearing the "sage of Lexington" firsthand was out of the question, owning a book of his sermons was the next best option.

McGarvey also had a sense of nostalgia. In his judgment, the most powerful preacher to emerge during the Restoration Movement was Moses E. Lard, who died in 1880. In his autobiography, McGarvey heaped praises on the oratorical prowess of his former colleague before observing, "not one of these sermons was ever written and not one is now preserved."[4] This apparent omission weighed on McGarvey and influenced his decision to sanction the 1893 volume. McGarvey's cherished friend was not far from his mind when he noted:

> I think that I should not have been moved to the preparation of the present volume, but for the deep regret which I have often experienced, in common with many thoughtful men, that some preachers whom we have known, and on whose lips we have hung almost entranced, have left behind them, when they departed this life, nothing but the faint remembrance of sermons which we should have been glad to read again and again, and which were worthy of being transmitted to many generations.[5]

Counseled by Tragedy

In addition to Lard's death, another incident prompted McGarvey to preserve items of interest. In 1887, McGarvey's Lexington home burned to the ground. Although no one was injured, the loss sustained was great. As he later summarized, "All manuscripts, letters and diaries, the accumulation of a life-time, together with nearly all of library and household furniture were lost."[6]

That McGarvey cherished his books is undeniable. In 1879, before leaving Lexington for a 6-month tour of the Holy Lands, he paused to address his library. "Good-by, my dear old friends; and if I never see you again, God bless you for the good you have done me and the happy hours we have spent together." [7] Not a decade later these books, as McGarvey lamented, "had gone up in smoke." [8]

Among the casualties of the blaze were over three decades of hand-written outlines. In discussing his method of sermon preparation, McGarvey mentioned these aids, again referring to their untimely demise:

> I adopted at the beginning of my ministry a systematic prepa-
> ration of sermons, by studying the subject carefully till it
> took shape in my mind, and then by making brief notes of
> its divisions and subdivisions which I committed to memory.
> But I left these written notes at home when I started to church
> to preach the sermon. *These skeletons, each of which filled a
> single page of note paper, I preserved till they were burned
> in the fire that destroyed my home* [emphasis added]. [9]

Thus, when McGarvey traveled to Louisville in 1893, any outlines he carried were "replacements" (i.e., rewritten versions of his previous notes and/or newer sermon material). Whatever became of these outlines? After losing priceless possessions once in a house fire, McGarvey likely took steps to protect future keepsakes from meeting a similar fate. Perhaps he entrusted them to family members upon his death in October 1911. Given his almost half-century connection with the school, it is possible they were immediately bequeathed to his beloved College of the Bible. It is impossible to trace their route with certainty.

An Unexpected Discovery

Alexander Fleming is reputed to have discovered penicillin quite by accident while working on another project. Although not as dramatic as the development of the world's first "wonder drug," the recovery of McGarvey's "lost" outlines was probably as inadvertent. During the fall of 2010, while researching a different aspect of McGarvey's career [10], I placed a telephone call to Carisse Berryhill, special services librarian at Abilene Christian University in Abilene, Texas. Berry-hill graciously pointed me to Barbara Pfeifle, then library director at

Lexington Theological Seminary, who in turn insisted that I speak with resident archival librarian, Charlie Heaberlin.

In talking with Heaberlin, he mentioned in passing that McGarvey was fond of writing everything out by hand – including his sermon outlines, some of which were in the library's possession. A few weeks (and a trip to Lexington) later, I was privileged to hold in my hands the very outlines McGarvey must have used during his famous visit to Louisville. For someone who appreciates the legacy of this venerable pioneer, it was a special moment.

Along with the outlines that were further expanded in his 1893 book of sermons, there were many others – outlines that presumably have seldom been seen during the last 100 years, if not longer. These relics of Restoration history should be of interest to serious students and are chronicled in this volume.

If McGarvey ever changed his estimate of sermon collections, we are not told. Although personal experience led him to counsel against imitation, he doubtless would have been gratified to learn of the influence his little book wielded. A quick glance at the first volume of N.B. Hardeman's *Tabernacle Sermons*, a work that eventually eclipsed McGarvey's in popularity, reveals how indebted the latter-day "prince of preachers" was to the 1893 edition.

At any rate, it is at least ironic that *Sermons Delivered in Louisville, Kentucky* proved to be the most profitable book McGarvey ever issued. As W.C. Morro relates, "He is supposed to have told his friends that it was the only one of his books that paid him any considerable sum in royalties."[11] Given his sense of humor, this unexpected twist surely was not lost on McGarvey.

In concluding the 1893 preface, McGarvey acknowledged that spoken material (such as that found in *Sermons Delivered in Louisville, Kentucky*) often lacks the polish of the written word. Although recognizing this deficit, he did not believe the spoken word was without merit. "If … [the sermons] smell less of midnight oil," he said, "the reader may be compensated if they shall have some of the freshness of morning dew."[12]

Similarly, it could be wished that full-length sermons were available to accompany the outlines here presented. It would be fascinating indeed to read the homilies of perhaps the greatest American-born scholar the church has ever produced. But if detailed expositions are denied us, blessings may still be enjoyed: echoes of truth that never fade, drops of dew from a distant land. ❏

Brandon Renfroe currently resides in Ashville, Ala., with his wife Amanda, and their three daughters: Breanna, Leah and Hadley. Brandon preaches for the Ashville Church of Christ and teaches environmental science in the Jefferson County School system.

Endnotes

1 This congregation is not to be confused with McGarvey's home congregation of the same name, the Broadway Christian Church in Lexington, Ky.

2 J.W. McGarvey, "Alexander Campbell, Barton W. Stone and Walter Scott," *Centennial Convention Report*, ed. W.R. Warren (Cincinnati: Standard, 1910). See also: http://www.mun.ca/rels/restmov/texts/wwarren/ccr/CCR15H3.HTM.

3 J.W. McGarvey, preface, *Sermons Delivered in Louisville, Kentucky*, by McGarvey (Cincinnati: Standard, n.d.).

4 J.W. McGarvey, *The Autobiography of J.W. McGarvey* (Lexington: College of the Bible, 1960). See also: http://www.mun.ca/rels/restmov/texts/jwmcgarvey/ajwm/AJWM00A.HTM. It seems, however, that at least one of Lard's sermons was preserved (see B.C. Goodpasture, "Christ's Conversation With Nicodemus," *Biographies and Sermons of Pioneer Preachers*, [Nashville: Gospel Advocate, 1954]).

5 *Sermons* preface.

6 *Autobiography*. Among the items lost was one in particular that those who appreciate Restoration history can only imagine the value of: a New Testament given to McGarvey by Alexander Campbell while McGarvey was a student at Bethany College. The inscription read that it was for "proficiency in knowledge of the Scriptures."

7 J.W. McGarvey, *Lands of the Bible* (1881; Indianapolis: Faith and Facts, n.d.) 387.

8 *Autobiography* 82.

9 W.C. Morro, *Brother McGarvey* (St. Louis: Bethany, 1940) 67-68.

10 The by-products of that research can be found in the appendix of this book in the form of several articles written about McGarvey and his role in Restoration history.

11 *Brother McGarvey* 178.

12 Sermons preface.

Old Testament

The Story of Balaam. Nu. 22-24; 2 Pe. 2:15

Int. An expressed need for more frequent discussion of passages ridiculed by infidels,— this one of them,— like that of Jonah liable to ridicule when the miracle is isolated — but we shall see it in its connections.

I. a. Wide-spread Belief in Enchantment,— or a specimen curse (White, 52) — b. Balaam's fame. Nu. 22:6,— c. Balak, his fear of Jehovah's people, his wish, his message. 22:2-6,— This an open issue between magic & Jehovah,— it called for decision.

II. How the Issue Met. a. Balak's messengers, rewards, & promises, & the effect on Balaam. b. Lord's alternative to hold him back, or let him go & to overpower him — latter alone decisive in sight of the enemy.— c. Effected, by (1st) refusal, 8-13, (2) Permission, but in words of his own. 20, (3) Knowing still his perversity, scares him out of it, by the angel & the ass. 22-35,— his Confession. 34,— his sin against God, & the ass — the rebuke from proper source — & God who could thus rebuke him is not to be disobeyed,— Thus far God is vindicated in mind of the enchanter, main vindication yet to come

III. The Final Trial. a. The Persons, the victims, the situation. 22:41-23:3.— the result. 7-12.— b. Another effort & result. 13-26,— c. A Third. 27-24:11,— Balak sees & acknowledges the triumph of Jehovah. 11: but for the ass Balaam would have added a curse.

Con. Story credible in itself — so made certain by the word of the Apostle,— Doubt nothing, but believe & obey.

The Story of Balaam
Numbers 22–24; 2 Peter 2:15-16

Introduction

An expressed need for more frequent discussion of passages ridiculed by infidels. This one of them – like that of Jonah liable to ridicule when the miracle is isolated – but we shall see it in its connections.

I. The Issue Presented

  A. Widespread belief in enchantment – a specimen curse (White, 52).

  B. Balaam's fame (Numbers 22:6).

  C. Balak, his fear of Jehovah's people, his wish, his message (22:2-6). This an open issue between magic and Jehovah – it called for decision.

II. How the Issue Met

  A. Balak's messengers, rewards and promises. The effect on Balaam.

  B. Lord's alternative to hold him back, or let him go and overpower him – latter alone decisive in sight of the enemy.

  C. Effected by …

    1. Refusal (Numbers 22:8-13).

    2. Permission, but no words of his own (v. 20).

    3. Knowing still his perversity, scares him out of it, by the angel and the ass (vv. 22-35), his confession (v. 34), his sin against God, and the ass – the rebuke from proper source – and God who could thus rebuke him is not to be disobeyed. Thus far God is vindicated in mind of the enchanter. Main vindication yet to come.

III. The Final Trial

  A. The persons, the victims, the situation (22:41–23:3). The result (23:7-12).

  B. Another effort and result (vv. 13-26).

  C. A third (27–24:11). Balak sees and acknowledges the triumph of Jehovah (24:11), but for the ass Balaam would have added a curse.

Conclusion

Story credible in itself – made certain by the word of the Apostle. Doubt nothing, but believe and obey.

Clearing the Way
Psalm 119:9

Introduction

Point in the question of the text – a way through the world, never trod before, to be cleared and followed by every one. How?

I. How It Is Often Done

    A. In early youth no attempt at it – thoughts and capers of mannish boys.

    B. Then, beating the bush without aim, until a path struck, one of many in wrong direction.

    C. Some choose the money path; drowning conscience. Some, the path of indulgence, ditto. Some, that of contention, fighting their way through life.

II. Consequences

    A. Reckless youth – so few young men in church, and so few in it of any worth.

    B. The vast number wrecked in health and character, and laid in early grave.

    C. Vast number of middle age hardened in sin.

III. True Way

    A. Only one Being sees all the way. He has given directions, hence the rule in the answer of text.

    B. It points to the goal, guards from every evil path, gives strength to cut through.

    C. It requires knowledge of the word; illustrate by compass at sea.

Exhortation

Read the Word – hold self steady to it.

Agur's Prayer
Proverbs 30:7-9

Introduction

Agur not known, but we accept his sayings (1) because endorsed by compiler of Proverbs, (2) because they agree with N.T., (3) because obviously true and wise.

I. Two Things Prayed For

A. Emphasized as of superlative value.

B. The first: negative, meaning of vanity of lies.

C. The second: also negative, but a positive result.

II. Wisdom of the Prayer

A. Seen in effect of riches. Why this effect?

B. In effect of poverty – in final effect of both (i.e., to despise God).

III. Wisdom From Other Considerations

A. These two hardest to reach by gospel, the rich the hardest – fortunate they are few. Should try to reach both, but not to neglect of the third class.

B. The prayer safest for our individual salvation – praying for it, regulate life accordingly. How we will look upon riches as we look back from the judgment.

Exhortation

Adopt the prayer, and give life to Jesus.

The Fiery Furnace
Daniel 3; Hebrews 11:34

Introduction

As compared with Jonah in the fish, the ass speaking audibly – like them credible only when viewed in its connections.

I. The Occasion

    A. The image and its dedication, design.

    B. The threat, and why. This a test of faith to Hebrews in office – if any bowed, a triumph of the new god.

    C. The trial, and the conduct of the three. Thus far their faith tested, but not their God.

II. Jehovah Put to the Test

    A. Accusation of the three and its purpose (Daniel 3:8-12).

    B. The issue made (vv. 14-15). God's power challenged, and this before the nations.

    C. The issue accepted (vv. 16-18). The alternative, save them from being cast in, or from the fire. The latter the greater.

    D. The result (vv. 19-27). The final effect on the nations (vv. 28-30) and on the new worship. All worthy of God, and affirmed by Paul.

III. The Preparation of the Three

    A. Impossible without previous training.

    B. The training while at college.

    C. How we shall be like them. If sinners hesitate and vacillate, no furnace of fire.

God Not Without Witness
Daniel 3:26-30; Acts 14:17

Introduction
Seeming neglect of heathen world in Jewish times – kept up witness
of works (text). Also more witness of word than we often think (e.g.,
plagues of Egypt; Jonah in Nineveh; Sennacherib's army and others;
proclamations of Nebuchadnezzar, Darius and Cyrus). Illustrate all
the latter by one.

I. The Fiery Furnace
A. Its incredibility with many.
B. If a naked fact without adequate cause and effects, incredible.
C. Like miracles of Jonah when properly understood.

II. Occasion and Purpose
A. Babylonian supremacy after fall of Nineveh, with king of
  boundless ambition and genius.
B. Attempt at one universal and binding religion by the great
  image and its worship (cf. attempts of popery).
C. Effect on true faith if effectual. A crisis demanding effectual
  and convincing interference by Jehovah.

III. God's Interference
A. In divine prescience, three Jews rulers of central province,
  Babylonia. They necessarily among the most conspicuous.
B. The vastness and gorgeousness and intelligence of the
  assembly – hence the temptation, but resisted.
C. Second chance offered, and results.
D. The attempt reversed, and Nebuchadnezzar a greater preacher
  than Jonah.

IV. Whence the Courage of the Three
A. The trial by the king's meat and wine.
B. If they had failed there, would have failed now – but true in
  small things made them so in great.
C. If sinners halt on threshold, never heroes in the fight.

New Testament

Mat. 16:13-20. How to Choose a Church. Feb. 12:18-24.

Int. Choice made on many grounds.

I Wrong Grounds. a. To be in fashionable Society. — b. To secure patronage in business. — c. Because father & mother were in it. — d. To be with husband or wife. — e. "Because I like it". — All these mistake the purpose of the Church, to save.

II. Right Ground, to secure right fellowship & government for final salvation. — a. The demands the church Christ built, described in texts. b Its Characteristics, (1) None entered it except by the Scriptural steps. Acts. 2. — (2) Had no creed by N.T. teaching but Scriptures. (2) No discipline but N.T. — (3) No name but Scripture names. (4) It is to be made perfect. Eph. 5:25. — c. Find this church & join it. — Whatever true of others, this certainly true.

Esch. No church till sins forgiven. Save yourselves.

How to Choose a Church
Matthew 16:13-20; Hebrews 12:18-24

Introduction

Choice made on many grounds.

I. Wrong Grounds

A. To be in fashionable society.

B. To secure patronage in business.

C. Because father and mother were in it.

D. To be with husband or wife.

E. "Because I like it." All these mistake the purpose of the church.

II. Right Ground – to secure right fellowship and government for final salvation.

A. The demands the church Christ built, described in texts.

B. Its characteristics.

   1. None entered it except by the scriptural steps (Acts 2).

   2. Had no creed but Scriptures.

   3. No discipline but N.T.

   4. No names but scriptural names.

   5. It is to be made perfect (Ephesians 5:27).

C. Find this church and join it. Whatever true of others, this certainly true.

Exhortation

No church till sins forgiven. Save yourselves.

The Good Confession
Matthew 16:13-20; 1 Timothy 6:12

Introduction

Universal to have some confession of faith. The one used by apostles and called "the good confession" ought to satisfy.

I. What It Is

    A. Seen in Matthew 16:13 (cf. John 18:37-38).

    B. In Romans 10:9-10.

    C. In 1 John 4:15. Its meaning.

II. Why "The Good Confession"

    A. Because of the honors and blessings indicated in citations just given.

    B. Because of benediction on Peter.

    C. Because first confessed by God Himself.

    D. Because it secures confession of us by Christ.

    E. It was response to what apostles preached.

    F. It was and is the distinction between belief and unbelief, and many have died for it.

III. Its Sufficiency

    A. Common objections met.

    B. If necessary to know all N.T. would be insufficient but then, nothing would be except examination on all.

    C. It binds to belief and doing of all as fast as we learn; hence it is sufficient.

Conclusion

All the universe shall confess; do it now while it can bring a blessing.

And Lose His Soul
Matthew 16:24-26

Introduction
A question of profit and loss. Gain, the whole world – loss, the soul.

I. What Is It to Gain Whole World?
    A. Whole world only three things: its property, its honors, its pleasures.
    B. The whole of each considered separately – with health and long life to enjoy them. Truly great gain.

II. What, to Lose the Soul?
    A. Not lose it as we lose property, but to "get lost" – equal to all of a sinner's eternity.
    B. Appropriateness of term "lost" to describe it.

III. What the Profit?
    A. All lost, as in bankruptcy.
    B. All previous gain now looked back on as loss; for all misspent and used for self-ruin.

IV. What, to Lose the World and Have Soul?
    A. All is now profit (e.g., Lazarus).
    B. Neither alternative: but gain a little, and lose or save soul.

Exhortation
As to save the soul is to save all, and the way clear, "save yourselves."

Is the Story of Jonah a Myth?

Luke 11:29-32

Introduction

This story usually the first point of skepticism and favorite point of attack. Position of some "evangelical" critics.

I. How the Main Facts Appear If Isolated

    A. That a man was thrown into the sea, swallowed by fish, thrown out alive.

    B. That one day's preaching in greatest city brought all to repentance.

    C. That gourd vine sprang in a night to shelter a man and perished in a night.

    D. This the way they appear to many, so would raising Lazarus till we know who did it and the occasion.

II. How They First Appear in Their Connections

    A. God's great purpose for Nineveh and the world.

    B. No way but by preaching – by preaching known to be from Him.

    C. The preacher chosen – greatness of his career as a prophet – but this not enough, the additional sign – fourfold purpose in latter: to bring Jonah back, to teach a personal lesson, to convert the sailors, to give a telling sign. These justify the miracle.

III. The Repentance and the Gourd Vine

    A. Preaching such a sermon by such a man, with such a sign, enough. Only gospel-hardened men could resist it.

    B. The further lesson needed by Jonah (Jonah 4:1-2) and by all Jews. The gourd vine the medium, and worthy of God.

    C. The affirmation of Jesus proves all.

Conclusion

The appeal of Jesus for repentance – His appeal to us still stronger, and our fate severer.

Is There Another Chance After Death?

Luke 16:19-31; 1 Peter 3:18-22

Introduction

Impenitent prone to saying time enough yet; and if it comes to the worst, there is a chance after death. What ground for this?

I. Does Text Offer the Hope?

   A. Affirms two things.

      1. That Christ preached to spirits in prison.

      2. That He preached in the spirit, and not in flesh.

   B. Does not affirm where or when, only that He was in spirit.

   C. Was in spirit twice: before advent and during the three days. If in latter, it was in the prison; if in former, before they died.

II. When and Where?

   A. Not a hint elsewhere that He did anything in the three days, except 1 Peter 4:6, whose meaning depends on this.

   B. There is assertion that God's spirit strove with them while living. Genesis 6 – what this spirit did Christ did in spirit. See John 1:1-3. This well known to Peter's readers and this the meaning.

   C. These antediluvians not the people for whom a second chance is claimed – but the reverse.

III. No Other Chance

   A. Seen first by rich man.

   B. By words of demons.

   C. By those in Hades coming to judgment to be condemned.

   D. By certainty that Jesus would have comforted us with some hint, if any chance.

Conclusion

This sermon throws us back to those before.

Why Baptize?
John 1:25

Introduction

Why the question put to John – why his answer? Same question to one another.

I. Our Answer

 A. Is it because it suits our sense of propriety?

 B. Is it because church requires it?

 C. Only right reason, God requires it.

II. Some Inferences

 A. If God requires it, how escape without it?

 B. If He requires it, requires it of some persons: who are they?

 C. Must do it as He requires it.

 D. Must expect the blessing He attaches – not otherwise.

Necessity for Faith
John 8:21-24

Introduction

[Robert] Ingersoll's remark about "He that believeth not" – not surprising that he should dislike it – but the passage is not alone.

I. Necessity Emphasized

    A. By Jesus. Text. Without faith, die in sins (v. 24), and never reach heaven (v. 21).

    B. Hebrews 11:6. If impossible to please God, impossible to be saved.

    C. His faith must be not only in God and in Christ, but in the Scriptures; for without last, former cannot be (John 20:31).

II. Why the Necessity

    A. Without faith in God, cannot please Him.

      1. Because will not do as He directs.

      2. Makes God a liar (1 John 1:10).

    B. Without faith in all three, no repentance: for nothing to make us realize our sin, nor the punishment of sin, nor the atonement – hence no salvation.

    C. Without it, no obedience, and this is fatal (John 3:36). No arbitrary requirement, but a necessity from our nature.

III. How Much Faith?

    A. Faith a growth – none have as strong before obedience as after.

    B. The need for it shows the amount necessary to begin (i.e., enough to induce repentance and obedience).

Applied

Do you believe you are a sinner? That perdition awaits you? That there is pardon through Christ? That you should obey Christ? Do you believe strongly enough to do it? If so, you have faith enough to be saved.

Paul Stoned at Lystra
Acts 14:19-20

Introduction

This is the greatest crisis in Paul's life – the cruelest treatment. What brought it about?

I. The Exciting Causes

    A. His work in Antioch, expulsion and indignant departure.

    B. Work in Iconium, and narrow escape.

    C. Work in Lystra till the attempt to worship him.

    D. News of this goes back to Iconium and Antioch, and the Jews, exacerbated came.

II. The Procedure

    A. Their hatred unaccountable, but their mode of persuading Lystrians obvious.

    B. Purpose concealed till opportunity comes, not anticipated by Paul – stones in hand – quick work, stoning and dragging out.

    C. Fearing higher authorities, Jews hasten home, satisfied and boastful.

III. The Sequel

    A. Paul's eyes opened, and what he saw. Who "the disciples" were, and how they found him.

    B. A night of weeping and nursing, and off to another city.

    C. Effect on Timothy, and on Paul.

Exhortation

As Paul followed Christ in suffering, let us follow him.

All Under Sin
Romans 3:9

Introduction

Why meetings, with their prayers and entreaties? Churches, with their labor and expense? The Bible, with the suffering of authors and defenders? The awful scenes of Calvary? The answer in our text: "all under sin."

I. Is the Answer True?

    A. Not of murderers, etc., but of all in all lands – to every one of us.

    B. The answer of our hearts, in solemn hours and before God – of every man, when disguise and pretense laid aside.

    C. The answer of the Bible.

II. Why So Serious a Matter?

    A. The pain that it gives the sinner himself – the murderer, the drunkard, the thief, the mere sinner.

    B. The pain it inflicts on others. Some examples.

    C. Impossibility of undoing the deed once done, or wiping out the guilt.

    D. Certainty that it must follow us into eternity: seen in the experience of the dying. Confirmed by God's Word.

Conclusion

If this life were all, the loudest call of the soul would be for deliverance from sin. How, we shall yet show; if any know it already, let them come.

Connection of Faith and Baptism

Romans 3:28; James 2:24

Introduction

Seeming contradiction in the texts. So in two doctrines, faith alone, and faith and baptism. Must find reconciliation.

I. How Reconciled

A. Only by ambiguity in one of the three leading terms.

B. Not in faith: there is one faith.

C. Not in justified: for justification before God can only be from sin.

D. Must be in works.

II. The Kinds of Works

A. Paul's, works of perfect obedience. See Romans 3:9, 19-20 – by these no justification because all have sinned.

B. James's, acts which exhibit faith: Rahab's (James 2:25) – Abraham's (v. 21).

C. Their connection with faith (vv. 22-23); and final conclusion (v. 26).

III. James' Conclusion Applied

A. The faith that saves us, faith in Christ. (References.)

B. This dead unless made effective by some act (i.e., dead as to desired effect: illustrated by cases of Abraham and Rahab, of woman with issue, of paralytic).

C. This faith made effective in baptism (Mark 16:16; Galatians 3:27-28). Real value of faith, that it leads to repentance, to baptism, and then to all the course of a faithful life. If these could be without it, it might be omitted.

Conclusion

If not enough faith to repent and be baptized, can only tremble like demons (James 2:19). If enough, come and tremble no more.

The Spirit of Christ
Romans 8:9-11

Introduction

Current use of the phrase – in this sense it is not found in N.T. Its meaning here – this meaning the key to that aimed at by the current phrase.

I. The Current Meaning

  A. Christ's extreme tenderness of feeling: shown in healing all, in receiving sinners, in sympathy.

  B. His meekness (i.e., no ambition, no resentment).

  C. His purity: seen in refinement of speech and of manner.

II. Defectiveness of This View

  A. All true – all necessary to high character, but insufficient – for ...

    1. It is negative – a character to be admired by good, but not feared by the bad, bad men praise Christ for it.

    2. It would make no leader of men – not rousing, not aggressive.

    3. If Christ and apostles no more than this, they would have been failures.

III. The Other Elements

  A. His hatred of hypocrisy – seen in Sermon on Mount and instances of rebuke.

  B. His fearlessness in speech and action and His zeal for right. (Instances.)

  C. His impartiality – disciples rebuked as promptly as enemies. (Instances.)

  D. His stern sense of justice – preceding and seen in final sentence on wicked.

  E. His prayerfulness – this the secret of perfect balance of character.

Conclusion

All this result of "spirit of Christ" in its true meaning. Let us have it more and more. Sinner, come and receive it.

How We May Know We Are Saved

Romans 8:16

Introduction
Uncertainty of many – wretchedness of it – confidence of apostles.
Same with us if we understand as they. The secret in the text.

I. The Text Explained
    A. Not one witness to our spirit – this the mistake: hence listen to own spirit and mistake it for Holy Spirit.
    B. Two joint witnesses: one testifying what a son of God is, the other what I am.
    C. These the only two.

II. Where and What the Testimony
    A. That of Holy Spirit, only in Scripture. Seen in passages of former sermons, believe, repent, confess, baptized.
    B. That of our spirit, consciousness as to each point. As result, I am or am not, and no uncertainty – nor ever can be.
    C. As to continuing a son, same test according to (v. 14).

Exhortation
If any doubt, it is on strict compliance. Illustrate by man sprinkled who doubted his baptism, but at rest after immersion – imitate him.

Gambling
1 Corinthians 9:24-27

Introduction
Rule as to selection of text – why not one containing present subject.

I. What Gambling Is
  A. Primary, playing for money, or other value.
  B. Betting on any result.
  C. Risking money on any uncertainty when no equivalent received (e.g., lotteries, raffles, futures, etc).

II. Its Illegality
  A. In all enlightened states, laws against – in some forums, a felony.
  B. Inconsistency of Kentucky law.
  C. Even raffles at church fairs indicted in Tennessee.

III. Why Made Illegal
  A. Essentially immoral to get something for nothing.
  B. Leads to greater wrong of basest frauds – seen in gambling devices and race courses.
  C. Condemned in 10th commandment.

IV. Its Prevalence
  A. Gambling dens.
  B. Pool rooms.
  C. Daily press.

V. How to Suppress It
  A. As citizens, jurors, etc., see to public opinion and enforcement of law.
  B. As Christians, put it out of church and family.
  C. Put down all exciting causes (e.g., card playing, billiards, horse racing at fairs).

Exhortation
Rebuke by example of heathen games in text. Play the game played by Paul in text.

The Lord's Supper
1 Corinthians 10:15-22; 11:17-34; Acts 20:7

Introduction

Most solemn event in history, the death of our Lord. Most solemn ordinance, commemorative supper. Must speak of it, think of it, and observe it as taught.

I. Its Name

    A. Only one given in N.T. (1 Corinthians 11:20).

    B. "The Communion," properly understood, justified (1 Corinthians 10:16).

    C. Not "the sacrament," "the eucharist."

II. Its Design

    A. A memorial – its adaptation to this – its blessedness as such.

    B. A communion – not with one another, but of the body and blood (i.e., a participation in the benefits of the body and blood as our spiritual food; 10:15-17).

    C. To lose sight of these facts is to partake unworthily (11:28-29).

III. Who Can Partake?

    A. None but baptized believers at first – so now.

    B. Even these if living wickedly, excluded – so now.

    C. No other restriction.

IV. How Often?

    A. No direction of Jesus.

    B. Inspired order seen (1 Corinthians 11:18-21; Acts 20:7). Early history.

    C. This admitted – hence this required.

Exhortation

To believers, regularity, solemnity – to unsaved, appeal from consideration that the event commemorated was for them.

Sanctification of the Church
Ephesians 5:25-27

Introduction

Strange that Christ should love the church, often so unlovely to us. Yet husband's love to wife feeble imitation of His love (v. 25). Reason, not what it is, but what it is to be. Yet even now it is not to be despised.

I. What the Church Is

    A. "Cleansed by the washing of water with the word" – meaning of this.

    B. No other society on earth thus cleansed.

    C. Some unclean have entered, but all the clean of earth are here.

II. What It Is to Be

    A. To be sanctified (i.e., to be holy and without blemish; 26-27).

    B. As consequence, "glorious church" – like white garment without spot or wrinkle.

        1. Glorious because of the admirable change.

        2. Because of admiration it will excite.

III. Process of Sanctification

    A. Word of truth the instrument.

    B. This administered by chosen men.

        1. Rulers called elders, overseers or bishops, pastors or shepherds – meaning of each, how they are to work, how they are to be regarded.

        2. Other teachers and preachers.

    C. According to Word, cutting off the disorderly.

    D. Deacons or servants, keeping all the work in motion by collecting and disbursing the means.

Exhortation

Keep Christ's aim before us and work for it with Him.

Appeal for Mission Church

1 Thessalonians 1:1-10

Introduction

Mission of the church to subdue the world to Christ. His plan of campaign to be followed.

I. The General Orders

   A. To all nations, but beginning from Jerusalem, and everywhere to Jew first.

   B. Reason, not partiality for Jew; but …

      1. Jerusalem and Jews best prepared.

      2. In this way, a base of operations for harder fields.

   C. So, every church worked first its own field (e.g., 1 Thessalonians 1:8).

II. Nature of Each Church Requires This

   A. It is a candlestick of gold – of gold, to indicate its value; a candlestick, because light-bearer; seven-branched, because its light, the perfect light of the gospel.

   B. Such light seen afar, but brightest nearby. Hence, church must turn its strongest light on its neighbors – they are best prepared.

III. How With Broadway

   A. The "work," "labor," "patience" (vv. 2-3), worthy of thanksgiving – especially in fields abroad.

   B. One thing lacking – a long delayed work at home – our origin a movement to spread in the city. We should lead in such movements.

   C. The work already done – the encouragement received – further delay forbidden. Every man to his duty – God looking down.

Lexington, March 31, 1889

The Church: The Pillar and Ground of the Truth
1 Timothy 3:14-15

Introduction

Connection between proceedings of the day and my subject. Train of apostle's thought (14-15).

I. The Imagery Explained

A. Truth compared to a building of which the church is pillar and ground. Not all truth, but truth connected with Christ (this seen in v. 16); meaning and connection of v. 16.

B. Figure of pillar explained.

C. Figure of ground explained.

D. Query: How this, when truth brought church into existence?

E. Illustrate by political parties and similar organizations.

II. How

A. By maintaining proclamation of truth – this the chief means (1 Corinthians 1:21). However criticized, a mighty power – to this end all houses like this.

B. By the work of other public servants – this specially referred to in context (v. 14; cf. 1-13)
1. By that of elders.
2. By that of deacons.

C. By mark of all the members (cf. Matthew 5:13-16).

III. Corollaries

A. Pillar of no error.

B. Work not done till all error corrected – this church to correct all error in this community.

C. This church must plant other churches.

Exhortation

We have the truth. Church's perpetuity assured by Christ, our individual fidelity the only thing uncertain. As preachers, elders, deacons, men, women, children, let us be faithful; the truth, the church, the dying world, the glorified Redeemer, our own souls demand it. Will penitent believers help us uphold the truth?

Evening of Opening Day of New House on Broadway, Sept. 20, 1891

The Invisible God
1 Timothy 6:15-16

Introduction

Items of the glory of Christ here set forth. Invisibility the crowning item – always true of God and now of Christ, not inconsistent with theophanies.

I. Apparent Disadvantage of This

  A. Difficulty of fixing thought and affection on invisible being and consequent desire of the visible.

  B. This the cause of all image worship, illustrated by Israel at Sinai and excuses for images given by heathen and Romanists.

  C. Result of the attempt, degradation of God, and then of man (Romans 1:23-24).

II. Real Advantages

  A. Visible things lose their power over our imagination (e.g., the sun, the ocean, the sky, the landscape). The invisible gains power with effort.

  B. The invisible, the most powerful (e.g., steam, electricity, air, gravitation). So all visible created by invisible.

  C. The invisible alone omnipresent – so with God.

III. Change at His Coming

  A. The word "no *man* hath seen or can [see]" (emphasis original). The invisibility pertains to the flesh.

  B. A change coming (1 John 3:2).

  C. No disadvantage then; for all will be perfect and eternal.

Exhortation

Come to the Invisible, see Him at last in glory.

What the Right Faith and Discipline?

2 Timothy 3:14-17

Introduction

Christianity being a life of faith and obedience, there is necessity for something to be believed, and some rules to observe (i.e., a creed and a book of discipline). Must save all who act it out, and reject none who are saved.

I. What the Creed?

    A. There is a belief necessary to salvation; it must include this. This is faith in Jesus, or the gospel concerning Him; this is the faith of the good confession.

    B. Faith in Him implies faith in all He said in person or through the apostles – hence belief of all the Bible.

    C. This divine, and meets the demands of a creed – no other does.

II. What the Rule of Discipline?

    A. If any human rules, may do wrong to enforce them; if divine, cannot.

    B. If human rules violated, may not be sin; if divine, must be.

    C. If divine rule given, it must be sufficient. It is declared to be (2 Timothy 3:14-17). This rule not the O.T. but the N.T.

III. Advantages

    A. It calls men, not to take our yoke, but yoke of Jesus.

    B. In seeking to follow and enforce it, must study it and learn it. This a blessed work.

    C. It can never divide true Christians.

    D. It judges here, that it may not condemn at last.

Exhortation

Come to the Bible, the light, the lamp – it tells us how to come, as seen in former sermons. It alone can guide us all the way.

Neglecting Salvation
Hebrews 2:2-4

Introduction

Paul's question an argument based on steadfastness of word spoken by angels, compared with greater certainty of that spoken to us. See its force by considering an example of former.

I. Lot's Elder Children and His Wife

    A. The cry of Sodom, God's talk with Abraham, and the mission of the angels.

    B. The work of the angels, the entreaties and escape of Lot, and fate of wife and city.

    C. Fatal neglect by his older children, partial neglect by wife, and results.

II. The Salvations Compared

    A. Heat from fire and by word of angels. This from eternal fire, and by word of Christ, apostles, God and Holy Spirit.

    B. The argument applied.

    C. If this from mere neglect, what from open wickedness?

Exhortation

Have already neglected much and long. Every hour the danger greater. "Remember Lot's wife," and follow Lot.

Sprinkling as Taught in the Bible

Hebrews 10:19-22

Introduction

Blood of Christ called "blood of sprinkling" (Hebrews 12:24), and we are come to it. We are elect according to foreknowledge of God "unto obedience and the sprinkling of the blood of Jesus Christ" (1 Peter 1:1-2). The manner of both writers implies ready understanding by their first readers, but not so with us.

I. The Fig[urative] (Hebrews 9:13-14)
  A. Blood and ashes typical of Christ's blood.
  B. As one cleansed the flesh, the other cleanses the conscience.
  C. The type was sprinkled; hence the name of the antitype: one literal, the other figurative. To trace out the comparison, must understand the literal.

II. The Literal
  A. Some of the blood always sprinkled.
  B. In consecrating priest, blood of bullock on him; and in cleansing vessels, blood of goat.
  C. Unclean from dead body, ashes dissolved in water.
  D. Leper, blood of bird on person, and by live bird. All this mysteriousness till Christ's blood called "blood of sprinkling"; these plain.

III. Why the Sprinkling and Why Ashes?
  A. Blood merely shed at altar a type, but inadequate: for first, used only there; second, used only then.
  B. Sprinkling, and especially bird's blood, typified universal diffusion; and ashes, perpetuity. Both ideas in "blood of sprinkling."
  C. Last two outside the camp, an effect of Christ's blood on sinner's conscience.

IV. Application in Text
  A. Drawing near to God set forth by analogy to Jewish cleansing.

B. The analogy: blood and ashes cleansed only when followed by bathing whole flesh; so, Christ's blood cleanses heart from evil conscience, when its first effect, penitence, followed by baptism. This, then, way to draw near, as taught generally in Acts.

Exhortation
Sinner knows of the blood shed; has felt its power. Has it brought him to repentance? If so, wash and be clean.

Law of Pardon
for the Christian
1 John 1:8-10

Introduction

Frequent objection that if baptism is for remission, it is so to
Christian as well as sinner and must be often repeated. Would be so
had God made it so, but God has made another law for Christians.

I. The Law

   A. Christians do sin (vv. 8, 10; 3:6, 9, not inconsistent with this).

   B. The condition, confession of sins (v. 9).

   C. The effect depends on blood of Christ (v. 7), He being now our
advocate with the Father (2:1-2).

II. Other Conditions

   A. As in case of confessing Christ (1 John 4:15), confessing sins is
not alone – there must be other conditions to make this one
effective.

   B. The conditions:

      1. Repentance (Acts 8:22; 2 Corinthians 7:8-10; 12:21;
Revelation 2:5).

      2. Prayer for forgiveness (Acts 8:22; James 5:16).

      3. Forgiving others if any have offended us. Lord's prayer
(Matthew 6:12-15).

   C. Combined, confession with repentance and prayer: to brethren
for sins against them and to God for all. This enables men to
daily obtain daily forgiveness, and last day last forgiveness.

Exhortation

To have Christian's forgiveness – to die forgiven – must begin with
sinner's forgiveness. All comes back to doctrine of previous sermons.

Young Men
1 John 2:13-14

Introduction

(In the interest of the YMCA) Scarcity of them in congregations – even here with all the colleges, 1,000 students besides home force, would suppose them largest element. Still scarcer in membership – many boys, but few young men.

I. The Ill Omen in This

    A. Effect on future membership.

    B. On future supply of officers and preachers.

    C. On financial strength.

    D. On preponderance of good or ill in community.

II. Our Duty in the Case

    A. Solomon's example in Proverbs.

    B. John's in text.

    C. Make special efforts according to special need.

III. Means of Success

    A. One a counter attraction against evil resorts, for leisure hours.

    B. One where work for other young men undertaken – work alone makes strength.

    C. This is a good YMCA with full equipment and zealous leaders. Its interest to church, to businessmen, to parents – renewed effort to improve and enlarge in Lexington.

Conclusion

Any young men ready to give strength to the Lord now and forever? Come.

Topical

Church Work.

I

That of the Elders.

1. Universality of ~~their~~ Appointment. _a_. In church of Judea. Acts. 11:30. – 15:6, – 21:18. _b_. In Pauline church. Acts. 14:23, – Phil. 1:1, – Titus 1:5. – _c_ In those of the Dispersion. Jas. 1:1 cf 5:14.

2. Their Work. _a_ As indicated by titles. Acts 20:17. 28, – Eph. 4:11. – _b_. By qualifications 1 Tim. 3:4, 5; Titus 1:9. _c_. By Precept. Acts 20:28; 1 Pet. 5:1,2. — _d_. By allusion. 1 Tim 5:17, – Heb. 13:7; 17. — The Sum: Ruling & teaching. Suggestions: _a_. Regular meetings. _b_. Division of work. 3. Discipline (over).

II.

That of Deacons.

1. Universality of Appointment. Acts 6:1-6. – Phil. 1:1; 1 Tim. 3:8-13. – ~~Why not so universal as elders~~?

2. Their work. _a_ As indicated by title, servants. — _b_. By statement. Acts 6:2,3. – what implied, — _c_. By qualification ruling & teaching omitted. 1 Tim. 3:8-13. — Note, Under oversight of Elders.

3. Were there Female Deacons? _a_ Bearing of "women". 1 Tim. 3:11. 12; Mr. 10:2; 12:15, 20; Acts 21:5, – _b_. Of διακονος Rom. 16:1. – c Origin of the order in 2d. Cent.

Suggestions: same as for Elders. – As to regular Church expense, apportionment.

Church Work

I. That of the Elders
A. Universality of Appointment.
  1. In churches of Judea (Acts 11:30; 15:6; 21:18).
  2. In Pauline churches (Acts 14:23; Philippians 1:1; Titus 1:5).
  3. In those of the Dispersion (James 1:1; cf. 5:14).
B. Their Work.
  1. As indicated by titles (Acts 20:17, 28; Ephesians 4:11).
  2. By qualifications (1 Timothy 3:2-5; Titus 1:9).
  3. By precept (Acts 20:28; 1 Peter 5:1-2).
  4. By allusion (1 Timothy 5:17; Hebrews 13:7, 17).
  5. The Sum: Ruling and teaching.
  6. Suggestions:
    a. Regular meetings.
    b. Division of work.
C. Discipline.
  1. Meaning.
  2. Included in teaching and ruling (cf. 1 Timothy 3:5; Titus 1:9).
  3. Involves withdrawal (2 Thessalonians 3:6; 1 Corinthians 5:9-13; Matthew 18:15-18; Revelation 2:2, 14-16, 20).
  4. Method of withdrawing (1 Corinthians 5:3-5). Public act of the church as a whole. Part belonging to elders? Way of procedure suggested.

II. That of Deacons
A. Universality of Appointment (Acts 6:1-6; Philippians 1:1; 1 Timothy 3:8-13).
B. Their work.
  1. As indicated by title, servants.
  2. By statement (Acts 6:2-3). What implied.
  3. By qualifications: ruling and teaching omitted (1 Timothy 3:8-13). Note: under oversight of elders.
C. Were there female deacons?
  1. Bearing of "women" (1 Timothy 3:11; cf. v. 12; Mark 10:2; 12:19-20; Acts 21:5).
  2. Of *diakonos* (Romans 16:1).
  3. Origin of the order in second century.

4. Suggestions: Same as for elders. As to regular church expense, apportionment.

III. That of the Evangelist

A. Titles and their meaning.

B. His work in the church (2 Timothy 4:5).
1. To set things in order (Titus 1:5).
2. To appoint elders (Titus 1:5; cf. 1 Timothy 5:22, 24-25). Distinction between appoint and choose.
3. Reprove, rebuke, exhort (2 Timothy 4:2) – publicly (1 Timothy 5:20) and privately (1 Timothy 5:1-3).
4. How to maintain authority (1 Timothy 4:12; Titus 2:15; vv. 7-8).

C. His relation to elders.
1. The same work except ruling.
2. Not to rebuke an elder (1 Timothy 5:1).
3. Meaning of 1 Timothy 5:19-20.

IV. That of Women (Why the Question)

A. As Seen in Examples.
1. Sapphira (Acts 5:1-11).
2. Mary, mother of Mark (Acts 12:12).
3. Lydia (Acts 16:15).
4. Priscilla (Acts 18:1-3, 18, 26; 1 Corinthians 16:19; Romans 16:3-5; 2 Timothy 4:19).
5. Phoebe (Romans 16:1-2).
6. Euodia and Syntyche (Philippians 4:2-3).
7. Lois and Eunice (2 Timothy 1:3-5; 3:14-15).
8. The women of Rome (Romans 16:6, 12).
9. Philip's daughters and the prophetesses in Corinth (Acts 21:9; 1 Corinthians 11:2-16).

B. As Taught by Precept.
1. To save disobedient husbands (1 Peter 3:1-5).
2. To teach the young women (Titus 2:3-4).
3. To be hospitable and benevolent (1 Timothy 5:9-10).
4. Women Speaking (1 Corinthians 14:34-37; 1 Timothy 2:11-14).

Conversion of Jailer

Introduction

Contrast with other individual cases in Acts. Subject to be treated same way.

I. Who He Was

  A. Roman, heathen, controller of criminals with all this implies.

  B. Had heard of Paul's preaching (16:30) but no heed to it – like many now, light present but not seen.

II. How the Lord Brought the Truth to Him

  A. Not as in case of Eunuch, Cornelius, Lydia, but a new and strange way.

  B. The steps in the process.

    1. Demon cast out.

    2. False accusation.

    3. Unjust punishment.

    4. Cruel order of imprisonment.

    5. More cruel execution of order – preacher now with jailer, but how different from other cases!

    6. Prayer, praise, earthquake, suicide, together again.

  C. On verge of heathen eternity, value of salvation realized.

III. Process of Conversion

  A. Preaching.

  B. Baptizing.

  C. Rejoicing.

Exhortation

Many like jailer at sunset, indifferent. All will be like jailer at midnight except they repent sooner – make no delay.

Conversion of 3,000

Introduction

Having seen what we must do to be saved by considering various passages, now examine some of the cases, beginning with the first.

I. The Persons and Their Transitions

    A. Devout Jews from every nation who had participated in killing Jesus.

    B. On morning of Pentecost, in usual state. In short time, full of distress and alarm, crying out. Before night, peaceful and happy Christians.

    C. Their experience recorded for our example.

II. The Process

    A. Their part in the crucifixion, the reports the third morning, their return after seven weeks.

    B. What brought them together in the temple, and their arrangement.

    C. The phenomenon explained, with no room for doubt.

    D. The story of Jesus, and the piercing of their hearts.

    E. Their question answered, and the exhortation to save themselves.

    F. They receive the word and are baptized.

III. The Items of Conversion

    A. They learn that the twelve are inspired, and must be believed.

    B. They hear the story of Jesus, and believe it.

    C. They learn what else to do, and do it.

Conclusion

As they saved themselves, save yourselves.

Discipline

Introduction

The two parties to the question. Our tendency toward Romish position.

I. Causes of Tendency
  A. Love of ease and popularity on part of officers.
  B. Desire for numbers and wealth, more than for souls.
  C. False interpretation of Scriptures (e.g., Parable of Tares).

II. Scriptures on the Subject
  A. As to the parable.
  B. As to other passages (Matthew 18:17; 1 Corinthians 5:9-13; 2 Thessalonians 3:6).
  C. The reason given (1 Corinthians 5:6-7).

Conclusion

Choose between Scripture and inclination, between God and Satan – path of duty the harder, but the short way and safe way. Individually, thank God for strict oversight, safest guide.

How to Study the Gospels

Introduction

What meant by study of Gospels. Necessity for such study as compared with that of all other books – "to know thee."

I. Study Them Singly

A. Every one a distinct conception, and distinctive representation of Jesus – this lost if the four as studied by a harmony, (e.g., taking four pictures and combining them).

B. Each to be known as a literary production.

C. Chronology – importance of – obtained only after preceding study and only by guidance of John.

II. Study Thoroughly

A. Learn minutest details.

B. Study by subjects.

C. Combine details of different writers.

III. Helps

A. [Flavius] Josephus, *Lands of the Bible* [by J.W. McGarvey], and pictures.

B. Consult no commentary till necessary.

C. No harmony till your own is made.

Conclusion

The task too hard? What can be too hard? Years I followed it? Our students make a start in it.

Lectures to Mountain Preachers' Institute

Public Worship

I. Order of It
  A. Hymns announced but not read. All quiet.
  B. Read Scripture. What kind of passage?
  C. Prayer. What petitions?
  D. Read hymn. What kind? Why read?
  E. Sermon.
  F. Lord's Supper. How conducted? What cups, etc.?
  G. Contribution. Why last?
  H. Closing hymn.

II. Preparation for It
  A. For the reading
    1. Get familiar with devotional passages.
    2. Select in advance.
    3. Study how to read it.
  B. For the prayer
    1. Learn how to pray (Luke 11:1; Romans 8:26).
    2. Think what to pray for each occasion. (Illustrate.)
  C. For reading hymn
    1. Study hymns much, and know the character of many.
    2. Memorize many.
    3. Practice reading.
  D. Invitation hymn
    1. Should fit the sermon.
    2. Select and announce before sermon.

III. Preparation of Sermon
  A. What is the purpose of a sermon?
    1. Not merely to teach.
    2. Not merely to excite feelings.
    3. To move to right action, by means of teaching and exhortation.
  B. First thing in preparation.
    1. Not text, or subject, but the particular aim.

2. This is to be determined by needs of hearers – if no particular needs known, aim at something all need.
C. A text containing the subject. Why a text? Why one containing subject?
D. Two kinds of sermons.
   1. Text sermon – divisions in the text. (Example.)
   2. Subject sermon – divisions according to natural parts of subject. (Example.)
E. After purpose fixed, text selected, and divisions determined, meditate till all takes shape. Illustrate by searching, ruminating. Make notes.

Second Part of Commission

I. Introduction.
   A. The two parts.
   B. How first part executed, seen in Acts; how the second part, seen in epistles.
   C. Our progress in the two.
   D. Jerusalem church the model (Acts 4:32-33). Items:
      1. Unity.
      2. Liberality.
      3. Power.

II. Unity
   A. Begins in the congregation: when each congregation united in Christ, we have the union prayed for.
   B. To be maintained by …
      1. Preaching for it.
      2. Praying for it.
      3. Settling disturbances as they arise (e.g., Acts 6:1-4, cf. 7).
      4. Scriptures are subject to be often discussed (e.g., Matthew 18; 1 Corinthians 6:1-11; 13:1-13.

III. Liberality
   A. Connection between unity and liberality.
   B. Extent of liberality in Jesus' church – not a blunder.
   C. Deficiency of it now.
   D. Evil effects of lack of it.
      1. On the person.
      2. On the church work.

3. On unity of church.
E. How to increase it.
  1. By preaching down covetousness, as did Jesus and apostles.
  2. By preaching up liberality.
  3. By exclusion of the extremely covetous (Acts 5:1-11; 1 Corinthians 5:9-13).
F. On this subject no undue severity – no flinching.

IV. Organization of Churches
A. Preachers' connection with this work.
B. Country life and country churches not known by apostles. Danger in these, weakness by crowding.
C. Purpose of organizing.
  1. Edification by keeping the ordinances.
  2. Conversion of sinners, by example and preaching.
  3. Training the young, saving the erring, and cutting of the dead members.
D. All in same organization.

V. Character and Work of Elders
A. Where new elders to be appointed.
  1. Negative requirements to be strictly observed (1 Timothy 3:1-7; Titus 1:5-9).
  2. The positive to be possessed in relative degree.
B. When there are elders already.
  1. Teach them to improve in all qualifications.
  2. If positively unfit morally, get them to resign.
  3. If no Scripture material, appoint none.
C. Most common defect, not want of qualifications, but neglect of duties.
  1. Of studying, so as to teach.
  2. Of admonishing the sinning.
  3. Of seeing to exclusion of the incorrigible – farce of title Shepherd.
D. When and how to withdraw from a member.
E. How elders to be corrected by preachers (1 Timothy 5:1).
F. Necessity for elders' meetings, and preacher with them.

VI. Character and Work of Deacons
A. Necessity for maintaining Scripture character (1 Timothy 3:8).
1. To obey the Lord.
2. To protect the church.
B. If one fails, what to be done?
C. Their work (Acts 6:2-3). Why serve Lord's table? Why considered financial officers?
D. How their work best done.
1. Regular meetings.
2. Division of labor.
3. Annual report.
4. Report to elders of delinquents.
E. Best way to collect money for regular expenses.
F. Lord's Day meetings.

VII. Appointment of Officers
A. How selected (Acts 6:1-4).
B. How appointed (Acts 14:23). Why the fast? The prayer? The imposition of hands?
C. Who to do the appointing (1 Timothy 5:22; Titus 1:5)? Must he appoint any elected (1 Timothy 5:22)?

VIII. Personal Character of Preachers
A. Keep good conscience, as guard to faith (1 Timothy 1:18-20). How evil conscience shipwrecks faith.
B. Avoid love of money (1 Timothy 6:3-11). How it works (v. 10). Why specially addressed to preacher.
C. Be an example in every virtue (1 Timothy 4:12).
D. Be devoted to the work (1 Timothy 4:13-16).
E. Avoid love of applause (2 Timothy 4:1-5). Not weathervane, but a breakwater. Not a lamb, but a shepherd. Not a rudderless ship, but a steamer.

July 22-25, 1890

Music in Christian Worship

Introduction

Nothing devised by art of man, so great power over feelings and imagination as music – power chiefly dependent on thoughts associated with it. It is for good or evil according to these (e.g., sacred music, martial, dance).

I. Its Use in Christian Worship

A. Vocal music for worship authorized in our rule of faith.

B. Its uses:
1. For God's praise (Hebrews 2:12).
2. For edification; hence, to be with the spirit and intelligible (1 Corinthians 14:14-17, 26). The method of edification, teaching and admonishing (Colossians 3:16). Three kinds of songs. (Illustrate.)

C. The effectiveness for these uses – the good accomplished by even one good voice – as to praise, the wonder that God is pleased with our songs!

II. Instrumental Music Not Authorized

A. The three ways of authorizing anything.

B. As to precept, none claimed.

C. As to precedent, none in church for 700 years.
1. One claimed in Judaism, but all this abolished.
2. One in Miriam's timbrel, but as well claim her dance.
3. One in John's visions: but as well the incense. It is vision and symbol, not reality.

D. As to implication, the word *psallo*. But:
1. This not supported by scholars.
2. Repudiated by Greek church.

III. Instrumental Music Forbidden

A. Not by express precept: for it is not mentioned but by implication.

B. Implied in abolishing Mosaic ritual, of which it was part.

C. In the apostles, reared to it under Judaism, worshiping in temple without it.

D. In prohibition of will-worship (Colossians 2:23; Matthew 15:9).

E. In that its fruits are evil:
1. Its history one of strife and division in all churches.
2. It violates law of Christian union.
3. It opens way for all Romish "helps" in worship.
4. Its use is abandonment of plea for primitive practice. This indictment sufficient.

IV. Personal Matters
A. Attempts to account for my opposition. My real education on the subject.
B. My rule as to connection with the organ stated.
C. My life-long desire for scriptural churches – my disappointment – my hope for Broadway – my final hope in God.

The Intellectual Study of the Bible

Introduction

Meaning of leading term – no absolutely intellectual study, for any study makes better or worse – means study for information as the primary purpose.

I. The Need of It

A. Deplorable ignorance of it among the young, the older, the educated, the YMCA, the preachers (some questions to audience).

B. Inexcusability, considering ...

1. The Book.

2. The characters it depicts, especially the greatest of all.

C. The fatal consequences.

II. How the Need Supplied

A. Individual study, as distinguished from mere reading.

B. Better study Sunday Schools.

C. Classes in YMCA.

D. Teaching in colleges.

E. More Bible in sermons.

F. In consciences.

III. Best Method of Study

A. If sufficient time devoted, as in Bible College, the books in order of time – every one for its contents, its structure, and its design – so all your life.

B. For the people, because of little time, and because most will know but little.

1. The career of Jesus.

   a. By its three divisions gathered from gospels and grouped.

   b. By miracles, parables, ethical teachings.

2. Acts, to learn careers of apostles, how sinners turned, how and where churches planted and organized.

3. Epistles, precepts, doctrine, history.

4. In all preceding, study O.T. references and then O.T. books chronologically.

Conclusion

If YMCA an instrument for bringing this about, its existence justified.

The Minister for Our Age

1. A man of faith (2 Timothy 1:3-5).
2. Full of scripture knowledge and hold to the pattern of sound words (2 Timothy 1:13).
3. Must hate covetousness (1 Timothy 6:3-11).
4. If young, must command respect by excellence of character (1 Timothy 4:12).
5. Model in deportment toward women and aged men (1 Timothy 5:1-2).
6. Must be industrious, and devoted (1 Timothy 5:13-15).
7. Careful in teaching (1 Timothy 4:16).
8. Must keep the brethren reminded of all duties and virtues (1 Timothy 4:6; 6:17).
9. Avoid all profane subjects.
10. "Fight the good fight" (1 Timothy 6:12).

Conclusion

Same as in Paul's day.

Appendix

Brother McGarvey
by Brandon Renfroe

A century has passed since the death of Bible scholar, preacher and educator John William (J.W.) McGarvey (1829-1911). However, his memory still remains vibrant among those connected with the American Restoration Movement.

From his earliest years, McGarvey seemed destined for greatness. His mother, Sarah Ann (Thomson) McGarvey, had been a student of Barton W. Stone; his stepfather, Gurdon F. Saltonstall, was a friend of Alexander Campbell, who dined in the family's home. To say the least, young McGarvey moved in rarefied air.

The association with Campbell proved influential, as McGarvey later attended Bethany College, graduating first in his class in 1850. After spending the next 12 years in Missouri, McGarvey relocated to Lexington, Ky., to work with the Lord's people – first at Main Street (1862-1867) and then at Broadway (1870-1881). The return to his native state was pivotal because Lexington became a hub for the brotherhood with McGarvey as its leading figure.

Central to the importance of Lexington was the presence of Kentucky University. In 1865, McGarvey there began what proved his life's work: teaching Sacred History in the College of the Bible. For the next five decades, many of the best and brightest in the Lord's church sat at the feet of the venerable "Brother McGarvey." Until his death in 1911, McGarvey was either teaching in the college or serving as its president.

Along with his fame as a preacher and an educator, McGarvey became well known through his many valuable writings. It is probable that no member of the church penned more for publication during the second half of the 19th century than he. From his legendary *Commentary on Acts* to the groundbreaking *Lands of the Bible*, along with his widely acclaimed works on higher criticism, "Little Mac" wielded a powerful pen.

Whether in words spoken or written, McGarvey's greatest legacy remains that of his conservative scholarship. In a time when liberal inroads were being made in the body of Christ – from the clamor for instrumental music to the denial of verbal inspiration – McGarvey stood as a gallant defender of righteousness and a staunch advocate for "the faith ... once for all delivered" (Jude 3). Eternity alone will reveal the victories for truth this mighty soldier won.

As with all good teachers, the lessons imparted by McGarvey were not reserved for his immediate pupils. Although hushed physically by man's mortal enemy (1 Corinthians 15:26), the spiritual voice of McGarvey still speaks (Hebrews 11:4). If we are wise – in a day when uncertain sounds often seem the loudest – we will listen carefully to what he has to say. ❑

Reprinted with permission Gospel Advocate *magazine, March 2011, pp 12-13.*

The McGarvey-Hayden Exchange: A Preview of Things to Come

by Brandon Renfroe

November 1864 was a notable month in American history. Abraham Lincoln was elected to a second term as president, easily defeating his Democratic opponent, George B. McClellan. Gen. William Tecumseh Sherman leveled much of Georgia on his infamous March to the Sea. And that same month, as the Civil War slowly began to wane, another battle brewed on a different front.

The weapons in this warfare would not assail physical strongholds, but "spiritual hosts of wickedness in heavenly places" (Ephesians 6:12; cf. 2 Corinthians 10:4). The conflict centered on the use of instrumental music in worship, and the spoils were invaluable because the souls of men were at stake.

The Instrument and Worship

There had been earlier skirmishes. In 1849, Alexander Campbell had made a passing reference to "singing choirs" and "instrumental devotions," labeling both as worship "by proxy." [1] Moses E. Lard, with characteristic flair, had bitterly denounced those seeking to introduce instruments as "defiant and impious innovator[s] on the simplicity and purity of the ancient worship." [2]

Many reputable historians have identified L.L. Pinkerton as the first to introduce instrumental music into a church connected with the Restoration Movement, referencing his actions at Midway, Ky., in 1859. The scholarly J.W. McGarvey, however, consistently pointed to 1869, with the Olive Street congregation in St. Louis, Mo., being the original offenders. [3]

As fate would have it, McGarvey fired the opening round in the printed war over instruments in worship. [4] Although others had assailed their use, McGarvey seems to be the first to formulate a precise argument in opposition. The magnitude of the moment was not lost on McGarvey; in recalling his article many years later, he described it as "the beginning of the discussion of the question among us." [5]

The battle unfolded on the pages of the *Millennial Harbinger*, the paper launched by Campbell in 1830 as the successor to *The Christian Baptist*. McGarvey's antagonist was A.S. Hayden, an Ohio preacher and composer 16 years his senior credited as "the author of the first compilation of church music published among the Disciples." [6] Their duel was waged from November 1864 to April 1865, and its ramifications are being felt still today.

Two Powerful Arguments

In his initial article, McGarvey advanced two arguments against the instrument, both based on the principle that the silence of the Scriptures is prohibitive. The first was derived from the apostolic invective against will-worship (Colossians 2:23). In detailing his opposition to all such forms of self-devised liturgy, McGarvey observed:

> [W]e cannot know what acts of worship are acceptable to God, except by express statements of revelation. ... We cannot, therefore, by any possibility, know that a certain element of worship is acceptable to God in the Christian dispensation, when the Scriptures which speak of that dispensation are silent in reference to it. To introduce any such element is unscriptural and presumptuous. It is will-worship, if any such thing as will-worship can exist. [7]

On these grounds, he concluded, we must reject the offering of sacrifices, the sprinkling of blood, the burning of incense, and the mechanical instrument in connection with Christian worship.

McGarvey then offered a challenge, which also contained the only method whereby his propositions might be falsified:

> If any man can mention an act or an element of worship now known to be acceptable to God, but not authorized by the New Testament, he will prove this argument against instrumental music to be invalid. I know not how it can be done in any other way. [8]

McGarvey then invited special attention to his second and more formal argument. The inspired men who instituted Christian worship, McGarvey observed, were reared under a previous economy. As Jews, the apostles naturally would have been inclined to perpetuate some items of temple worship, and under the guidance of the Holy Spirit, some aspects of Jewish liturgy were in fact retained. Others, however, were discarded. The implication was clear:

> Seeing, now, that all the acts of Jewish worship had been appointed by divine authority, the only conceivable reason why any of them were discontinued must have been that they were unsuited to the Christian worship. The very fact, therefore, that any part of Jewish worship was discontinued by those who organized the Christian church, is a direct condemnation of it by the Spirit of God, as unsuited to the new institution. But the use of instrumental music is an element of Jewish worship which was thus discontinued, and therefore, it is condemned by the infallible authority of the Spirit. [9]

If the "Discontinued by Design" argument was valid, McGarvey insisted that "nothing more need be said against instrumental music by lovers of the truth; and certainly nothing more should be said in their favor unless it can be set aside." [10] He closed by expressing his wish that the question be "fully discussed and finally settled." [11]

"Specious, Suspicious, Sophistry"

A.S. Hayden took up McGarvey's gauntlet in January 1865 with one caveat: he claimed not to be a proponent of the instrument. "I am no advocate of that practice," he averred. [12] His stated purpose for entering the fray was "not to defend the practice ... but to test the argument"

– although he would give a different reason later in the exchange.

The elder Hayden was forceful in his criticism, calling McGarvey's argumentation "specious" and his conclusion "suspicious," even going so far as to label it "sophistry." He was particularly perturbed by what he described as the "conclusion based on silence" set forth in McGarvey's second argument.

Although he conceded that "all parts of the Jewish economy passed into disuse," Hayden did not believe that New Testament silence was the determinative factor in their exclusion. Nor did he believe that instrumental music might appropriately be classified with elements of the Law of Moses, so that if incense was excluded by McGarvey's silence argument the instrument still was not. He chided McGarvey: "Where is the record that it was ordained in the law? Moses is 'silent' about it."

A Survey of Hayden's Blunders

Hayden did not have to wait long for McGarvey's rejoinder, printed in the February 1865 *Harbinger*. After renewing his unheeded challenge for the identification of a current act of acceptable worship not authorized by the New Testament, McGarvey called attention to the first of several blunders committed by Hayden.

McGarvey observed:

> You object to my reason for "the disuse of *incense, lamps, and priestly robes*"; but in giving what you style "the New Testament reason for their disuse," you demolish instrumental music as effectually as my own argument would have done. You say, "These, and other, and *all parts* of the Jewish economy passed into disuse, because that institution decayed, waxed old, and was ready to vanish away." Now the use of instruments in worship was certainly *one* part of that economy. When, therefore, "*all parts* of that economy passed into disuse," what became of instrumental music? The blows of your own logic have demolished it. [13]

Given Hayden's misstep, McGarvey could not resist a good-natured gibe at the instrument: "The poor thing is certainly in a bad way, when those who strike in its defense cannot avoid knocking it in the head."

As McGarvey next explained, his opponent fared no better in the attempt to overthrow the second silence argument:

> In attempting to put my argument into a syllogistic form, you state the major premise as follows: "Practices ordained in the law of Moses, on which the New Testament is silent, are condemned by the Holy Spirit." You then say, "Instrumental music is not of that category." You deny that it was either "ordained in the law," or "incorporated into the ancient institution, so as to bring it under the class of reasoning here discussed." Now if this is true, it follows that instrumental music in worship never was divinely authorized even among the Jews; that it was will-worship with them; and that with us it is a wicked imitation of a Jewish corruption. Surely, Bro. Hayden, yours is a two edged sword, and its back strokes are the most fatal. [14]

Whether one believes instrumental music was divinely authorized among the Jews is immaterial. If it was, New Testament silence nevertheless forbids it. If it was not, then it was will-worship and to incorporate it today is an apostasy of an apostasy! In this, McGarvey revealed Hayden to be perhaps more lyricist than logician.

A Telling Revelation

Hayden offered his final response in April 1865, and in so doing he disclosed his true feelings regarding the instrument:

> To my mind it is self-evident that no divine legislation was ever made touching the subject; and that any attempt to rank it among questions of law, as regulated by divine enactment, is far outside the range of truth and sound judgment in the case. It must be left among the subordinate regulations to be managed by the good sense of the brethren. [15]

Was this what Hayden meant by his earlier claim that he did not advocate the instrument? If so, surely he could not have been surprised when concerned brethren called him into question. As it turns out, what motivated Hayden was not truth but rather potential consequences.

In a paragraph he called special attention to, Hayden charged:

Granting the work done, the argument sound, the conclusion vindicated: what then? That the use of instrumental music is unauthorized? Nay, far more. It is condemned by the Holy Spirit, condemned also by God our Father; by Christ our Savior; condemned by prophets and apostles, by the angels, and by all the universe of good beings. ... And then what? We are bound by an authority we dare not resist, to condemn, reject, eject, every church, every member who persists in the flagrant sin. Then come alienation, bitterness, strife, ill will, dissension, schism. This is the inevitable result. I see no avoidance of this train of dire calamities which your argument, sustained, hurries along, and hurls over our churches like blazing coals of fiery strife. [16]

We Must Obey God

If Hayden sought to elicit sympathy from McGarvey, he was unsuccessful. Because the silence of the Scriptures forbade the use of the instrument, to rail against any potential ramifications was "to fight against God" (Acts 5:39). McGarvey would not fail to point this out to his colleague:

But why should you shrink from these consequences? If "alienation, bitterness, strife," etc., are to result from a "*sound argument*" with its "conclusion *vindicated*," showing that God and Christ, and prophets and apostles condemn a practice, are we, for this reason, to let that practice go unrebuked? Is brother Hayden the man to shrink from maintaining arguments which show such things, in order to avoid dreaded consequences? With all his gentleness, he is one of the last men to occupy such a position. [17]

Modern "Haydens"

Thus ended the first round of verbal jousting. Although others would join the fray in subsequent issues of the *Harbinger*, McGarvey was finished for the time being. [18] Another work by Hayden in 1868 would spur a brief exchange, [19] causing a concerned McGarvey to urge his brethren "to open our eyes and try to see whither we are drifting." [20]

Hayden was slowly chipping at the foundations upon which the Restoration Movement had been built, all the while pledging allegiance to its principles and expressing dismay at any "dogmatist" who would dare question his soundness. When he died, he left a multitude of like-minded brethren the blueprint for advocating and implementing change in the body of Christ.

There are still "Haydens" today and those eager to applaud them. How beneficial it would be to learn from history that what is often championed as progressive and forward-thinking is little more than old lies in new robes. Sadly, the principle of silence continues to be the stone many fall upon, breaking themselves in pieces (Matthew 21:44). ❑

Reprinted with permission Gospel Advocate magazine, March 2011, pp 14-16.

Endnotes

1 *Millennial Harbinger* (May 1849) 300. Ironically, this was in a brief piece advertising A.S. Hayden's hymnal *The Sacred Melodeon.*

2 Moses E. Lard, "Instrumental Music in Churches and Dancing," *Quarterly* (March 1864) 331.

3 J.W. McGarvey, *Autobiography of J.W. McGarvey* (College of the Bible, 1960) 61. See <www.mun.ca/rels/restmov/texts/jwmcgarvey/ajwm/AJWM01.HTM#Pg61>; J.W. McGarvey and F.G. Allen, *What Shall We Do About the Organ* (1903) 3. See <www.bible.acu.edu/crs/doc/mcal.htm>. It is possible this curious difference may be accounted for in that McGarvey was referring specifically to the first instance of an organ, typically introduced into the corporate worship, as opposed to the melodeon, frequently introduced into "Sunday Schools." At any rate, McGarvey was acquainted with Pinkerton, as both served on the Kentucky University faculty during 1865. (See also McGarvey, *Autobiography* 31.)

4 W.C. Morro, *Brother McGarvey* (Bethany Press, 1940) 136-137.

5 McGarvey, *Autobiography* 61. See <http://www.mun.ca/rels/restmov/texts/jwmcgarvey/ajwm/AJWM00A.HTM>.

6 *The Living Pulpit of the Christian Church*, ed. W.T. Moore (Cincinnati: R.W. Carroll Publication, 1868) 495-496. See <http://www.therestoration movement.com/hayden,as.htm>.

7 "Instrumental Music in Churches," *Millennial Harbinger* (Nov. 1864) 512.

8 "Instrumental" 513.

9 "Instrumental" 513.

10 "Instrumental" 514.

11 "Instrumental" 514.

12 *Harbinger* (Jan. 1865) 40.

13 *Harbinger* (Feb. 1865) 89.

14 *Harbinger* (Feb. 1865) 90.

15 *Harbinger* (April 1865) 185.

16 *Harbinger* (April 1865) 185.

17 *Harbinger* (April 1865) 188.

18 Many of McGarvey's future articles on instrumental music would be published in the *American Christian Review*.

19 "Expediency and Progress," *Millennial Harbinger* (Jan. 1868) 135-144.

20 "Brother Hayden on Expediency and Progress," *Millennial Harbinger* (April 1868) 216.

J.W. McGarvey and the Tragic Tale of Broadway

by Brandon Renfroe

An old maxim warns, "Those who do not remember the past are condemned to repeat it." That the sentiment is true needs little demonstration. It is verified time and again by human experience, and it is confirmed by Scripture (cf. Hosea 4:6; 1 Corinthians 10:6).

Although done to one's own peril, the neglect to study history is common. For many, the subject comes garbed in drab apparel with little to commend it to modern sensibilities. Viewing it as an unending torrent of dates and facts, the public drowns in a sea of mental oblivion. The attitude is unfortunate and overlooks one crucial point: History is about people, and people are rarely boring.

Few men associated with the Restoration Movement have been studied more carefully than J.W. McGarvey. The reason: McGarvey was an outlier, one of those intriguing individuals who defy easy characterization. A former student described him as "an apostle born out of due season." [1] A biographer chosen by McGarvey's family unsympathetically portrayed him as a "legalist." If not always in agreement with his theology, men on both sides of the theological spectrum respected McGarvey – a rare tribute, indeed.

One chain of events from the life of McGarvey has received

comparatively little attention, yet stands as a powerful microcosm of the turmoil faced by the body of Christ at the turn of the 20th century. In fact, it might be suggested that the events surrounding McGarvey and the Broadway Christian Church [2] encapsulate, in several epic acts, the great struggle faced by the Lord's people in all times. Although the plot could have been taken from an ancient Greek tragedy, it is a thoroughly American tale and one worthy of a modern audience.

The Main Street Years (1862-1867)

McGarvey was a native of Kentucky, but spent much of his youth outside the Bluegrass State. He lived for nearly a decade in Illinois before enrolling as a student in Alexander Campbell's Bethany College in 1847. After his graduation in 1850, the 21-year-old McGarvey moved to Missouri where he later married the former Atwayanna Hix. [3] The couple resided in Dover, Mo., for the next nine years before the Civil War changed their lives in a way they could not have anticipated: It brought McGarvey back to his "Old Kentucky Home."

As was true of most of the pioneers, McGarvey was a pacifist, urging that Christians should remain aloof from carnal conflicts. Not all shared this belief, of course. Among them was Winthrop H. Hopson, minister for the Main Street church in Lexington, Ky. Hopson had southern leanings that were not appreciated by the northern sympathizers in his congregation. In an effort to keep the church from splitting, Hopson resigned and recommended McGarvey for his position. [4]

McGarvey's neutrality was just the balm the warring congregation needed. Although largely unnoticed, it may be that the greatest feat of McGarvey's ministry was his masterful handling of this potential powder keg. The congregation not only survived, but thrived. When McGarvey arrived in Lexington in 1862, Main Street was the fourth largest congregation of any church in the city. By the time he resigned as its minister, it would be the largest. [5]

The years spent at Main Street were fruitful in many ways. In 1863, McGarvey completed his renowned *Commentary on Acts*, a volume later described by Guy N. Woods as "the greatest *uninspired* work ever written." [6] He also would pen the first article to appear in the *Millennial Harbinger* on the topic of instrumental music. The November 1864 essay signaled troubled waters were ahead – seas so perilous not even the capable McGarvey could navigate them.

But it was the relocation of what then was called Kentucky University from Harrodsburg to Lexington in 1865 that would mark a turning point in McGarvey's career. After turning down multiple overtures from Campbell to teach in Bethany College, McGarvey accepted a position in the Lexington school. In addition to his duties at Main Street, he was now "Professor McGarvey" in The College of the Bible, an arm of the new university.

It was not long until McGarvey's course "Sacred History" made more demands on his time than his ministerial duties would allow. Reluctantly, "and against the earnest desire of the church," [7] McGarvey resigned from the Main Street pulpit in 1867. He continued to serve the congregation as an elder, however, and his association with the church would soon place him behind another pulpit – the one from which he would wield his most significant influence.

On Broadway (1870-1881)

McGarvey was followed at Main Street by L.B. Wilkes, and the church continued to flourish. Soon, "overflow meetings" were held in Odd Fellows Hall, which once had been an opera house. The first of these was on Jan. 1, 1870, with McGarvey delivering the inaugural sermon. The local newspapers chronicled the event, reporting that "attendance was fine considering the deep snow." [8]

A few months later, a building was purchased to accommodate the overflow. It soon became apparent that a separate congregation had formed, and on July 16, 1871, 128 men and women formally placed their membership. The Main Street congregation had given birth to a daughter: the Broadway Christian Church.

Because the newly formed church was decidedly smaller than its parent, McGarvey agreed to serve concurrently as both its minister and as an elder. For the next four decades, McGarvey's place in Lexington – and the brotherhood – was second to none. As W.C. Morro observed, "From this time forth his classroom in the College, the pulpit of the Broadway Church, and the study where he wrote his books and articles, became the three centers of his activity and influence." [9]

A dozen years at Broadway would see its membership swell to almost 400, [10] causing McGarvey again to tender his resignation, which took effect on Jan. 1, 1882. He would continue to serve Broadway as an elder for an additional two decades.

Although he abdicated the Broadway pulpit, McGarvey continued to preach at other venues as his schedule allowed. It was at Louisville – at another Broadway church – that McGarvey in 1893 delivered a series of sermons that later would be published in book form. In penning the dedication, McGarvey showed that his own beloved Broadway was foremost in his heart:

> To "The Broadway Church," Lexington, Ky., in whose pulpit nearly all of these sermons were originally delivered; in whose service I have spent the most useful years of my life as a preacher, and among whose members I count many of my warmest friends, this volume is affectionately inscribed as a token of gratitude for many expressions of Christian fellowship. [11]

A brief historical sketch of the Broadway church authored by McGarvey in 1897 shows that neither his affection nor his optimism had abated. By then, the congregation had grown to 900 members – more than twice the size it was when McGarvey resigned as minister. Writing as a proud elder, he sounded a positive note:

> Her devotion to the faith and practice of the primitive church, for the defense and maintenance of which she has ever stood, knows no abatement. ... She has a large attendance every Lord's day which nearly fills her large auditorium; her Sunday-school is large and growing; her prayer-meeting is largely attended; and her young people, in their special lines of work, are active and zealous. She has every reason to thank God, and take courage. [12]

Despite his boast, McGarvey could not have been unaware that trouble was lurking. The Main Street church, for which both he and Moses E. Lard had once labored, decided to incorporate an organ into its worship in 1887. [13] By this time, Broadway was the only prominent congregation in Kentucky that did not use an instrument in its public worship. The winds of apostasy were blowing, and McGarvey's cherished Broadway would not go unscathed.

From Triumph to Tragedy (1902-1903)

The 50th anniversary of McGarvey's ordination as a minister was celebrated on Sept. 21, 1902. To commemorate the occasion, he preached before a large Broadway audience and closed the service by resigning from the eldership. He was 73 years old and, by his own admission, "could no longer hear sermons or prayers or understand singing without a book in hand." [14]

For half a century McGarvey had defended the Bible with eloquent tongue and brilliant pen against any who would assail it. The church at Broadway had the benefit of his wisdom and leadership for more than three decades as McGarvey shepherded the flock since its inception in 1870. They were a people most blessed.

Nov. 2, 1902

Less than two months after McGarvey resigned, a bombshell was dropped. On the morning of Nov. 2, 1902, it was announced that the use of the instrument would be put to a congregational vote the next Sunday. It took just 42 days after McGarvey's resignation for the Broadway leadership to stray from the course its most prominent member had charted.

Several factors were likely involved in this seemingly abrupt shift. Years earlier, the leadership of the Broadway congregation had decided to allow organs into their "Sunday School." It cannot be denied that this action, in which McGarvey apparently acquiesced, [15] set a dangerous precedent that ultimately opened a door they were unable – or unwilling – to close. On his part, McGarvey placed the blame on a weak Broadway pulpit, stating that in his absence "it was occupied by brethren who had no scruples on the subject," and as a result, "the private members were left to drift on the current of surrounding influences." [16]

With McGarvey serving as president of a Lexington college, [17] the unfolding drama was deemed newsworthy by the local papers. On three occasions they gave the church happenings at Broadway front-page billing. In the estimation of the *Lexington Leader*, McGarvey's influence was all that had prevented an anxious membership from incorporating the instrument years earlier.

Phrased in the sectarian vernacular one would expect, it reported:

> For years there has been a sentiment in favor of an organ. This has been combated by President McGarvey, who believed that the introduction of any musical instrument into worship was contrary to the teachings of the Bible and he has written and uttered much on this subject. Nearly all churches have adopted the organ, and this step by one of the largest churches of the denomination of Disciples, after holding out against instrumental music for over thirty years, is notable.[18]

Although he later would write of being "painfully disappointed"[19] at the sudden turn of events, McGarvey was not surprised. Earlier that spring, the Broadway elders had shared with their colleague that the "fixed purpose of an overwhelming majority [was] to introduce an organ." Anticipating what was to come, they asked McGarvey to either reconsider his long-held position or else "content himself with a mere public protest, and acquiesce in the change."[20]

This McGarvey could not do. On the same day the initial announcement was made, McGarvey requested letters of transfer from the Broadway church for him and his wife.[21] The die was cast, and the wise professor knew that further protest would be futile. McGarvey immediately began attending the Chestnut Street church, which did not use the instrument and with which he was associated for the rest of his life.

Nov. 9, 1902

On the day the Broadway vote was to be taken, brethren sympathetic to McGarvey proposed a resolution that would have postponed the matter indefinitely. The resolution was defeated 140-112, with many members not present or else refusing to vote.[22]

Charles J. Bronston, a Broadway member opposed to the organ, argued that a small percentage of brethren should not be allowed to decide the question for the entire congregation. In a membership approaching 1,000 individuals, he noted that only a fraction were present and voting. He then moved to postpone the organ vote for two weeks, and the motion narrowly passed. [23] The *Lexington Herald* described the day's events as "a victory for the anti-organ faction." [24]

Nov. 16, 1902

Shortly after the announcement on Nov. 2 that Broadway would vote on the organ, the *Lexington Leader* solicited from McGarvey a written defense of his position for publication. This he politely declined, although he indicated he might be willing to accede to their request when the matter was settled (which McGarvey believed would be Nov. 9). [25]

Granted the unexpected interlude, McGarvey decided to take advantage of the opportunity. In an article published in both the *Lexington Herald* and the *Lexington Leader* on Nov. 16 (see page 85), he made one last attempt to articulate his position before the final vote was taken.

Nov. 23, 1902

On the morning of the much-anticipated vote, Broadway was crowded. After an abbreviated service, John C. Willis, chairman of the elders, made a statement to the membership:

> Broadway must be a unit. No matter how the question is decided, every member should now make up his mind to abide by the will of the majority. There must be no disintegration, but we must be satisfied with the results. Let us forget the dissension, factions and discontent of the past, and go forth to meet the future strongly. [26]

The statement by Willis, if noble to some, might seem less than genuine to others. Of course it is easy to be magnanimous when one is reasonably certain the outcome will go in his favor. [27] Minister Mark Collis joined Willis in urging the members to "receive the decision without any expression of approval or regret." [28]

Although it took more than an hour for the votes to be tabulated, few could have been surprised when the final results were revealed. By a vote of 361-202, the instrument was voted into the Broadway church. [29] "Organ Side Wins" greeted the readers of the *Lexington Leader* the next day.

The Broadway brethren did not immediately inform McGarvey of their decision. After attending Sunday morning services at Chestnut

Street, however, he was approached by the *Lexington Herald* for comment. Unaware of the outcome, he learned the result from a reporter. In response, he said:

> I have no statement to make. I have not thought of anything I ought to say, except that I had expected this result, though I did not know how the vote would stand. I regretted that the personal element ever entered into the discussion, and that any one should have voted on the question on account of my stand. Several members had told me that they did not expect to vote, and this was indicated by the number of ballots cast. [30]

Although reserved in his public comments, the old soldier was scarred by Broadway's betrayal. In fact, three years later the wounds still seemed fresh. Writing in the more modest third person he revealed:

> This dereliction on the part of the church to which he had given the best work of his life as a preacher and an elder, and which still contained a large number of his most devoted friends, was a severe blow to his feelings but he swallowed his disappointment, and went quietly on in the Chestnut Street Church, which received him with open arms. [31]

Sad Postscript

The Broadway members followed through with their intentions, incorporating the instrument into their worship services early in 1903. As the *Lexington Leader* reported, after adding an organ for the "Sunday school room," the brethren planned "to place a handsome pipe organ in the auditorium." [32] Its price was $2,500 [33] – no small sum for the day – but many would agree it cost much more.

As often related, when McGarvey died in 1911, the Chestnut Street church was too small to house the mourners who would attend his funeral. With Broadway undergoing repairs, services were held at the Central Christian Church, and the organ was used. "This is a great wrong," one woman was heard to say.

The Broadway church still stands in Lexington, Ky. For her first three decades, a cappella singing was standard. Today, classic worship at

Broadway requires the use of a pipe organ. For those with more modern tastes, a contemporary service is offered as well.

On a wall just outside its stately auditorium, portraits of a dozen former ministers are prominently displayed. The first of these is of the great J.W. McGarvey, who has watched symbolically for more than a century as apostasy, like a tidal wave, has swept through our great brotherhood. To anyone who will listen, he delivers a message: How quickly we forget. ❑

Reprinted with permission Gospel Advocate magazine, March 2011, pp 17-21.

Endnotes

1 Hugh McClellan, *The College of the Bible Bulletin* (Lexington: May 1929) 40.

2 It should be noted that "Christian Church" and "Church of Christ" largely were used without distinction during the early years of the Restoration Movement. "Christian Church" was intended to convey the church composed of Christians; it did not have the sectarian connotation now associated with it.

3 The spelling of her name varies from source to source; this is from McGarvey's *Autobiography* (19). She would be his companion for 58 years, dying just over five weeks after McGarvey on Nov. 12, 1911.

4 W.C. Morro, *Brother McGarvey* (St. Louis: Bethany Press, 1940) 78.

5 J.W. McGarvey, *Autobiography of J.W. McGarvey* (College of the Bible, 1960) 27-28. See <http://www.mun.ca/rels/restmov/texts/jwmcgarvey/ajwm/AJWM00A.HTM>.

6 Guy N. Woods, *Questions and Answers*, vol. 1 (Henderson, Tenn.: Freed-Hardeman University) 313.

7 *Autobiography* 33.

8 *The Lexington Observer & Reporter* (Jan. 5, 1870).

9 Morro 205.

10 *Autobiography* 34.

11 J.W. McGarvey, *Sermons Delivered in Louisville, Kentucky* (Lexington: Guide Printing & Publishing, 1894).

12 J.W. McGarvey, *The Church Record* (New York: Church Record Publishing Company, 1897) 41-42. See <http://www.mun.ca/rels/restmov/texts/jwmcgarvey/etc/BCCHS.HTM>.

13 Morro 144, 264.

14 *Autobiography* 59-60.

15 Yet, in an April 1868 article in the *Millennial Harbinger*, McGarvey had written: "I need not pause here to argue, to any thoughtful person, that if it is wrong to use the organ in the church, it is wrong to train the children to use it in the Sunday School."

16 *Autobiography* 64.

17 McGarvey was president of The College of the Bible from 1895-1911.

18 "Quits Church," *Lexington Leader* (Nov. 3, 1902).

19 *Autobiography* 64.

20 *Autobiography* 64.

21 Morro 221.

22 Morro 222.

23 "Vote on Organ," *Lexington Leader* (Nov. 10, 1902).

24 "Contest Develops Over the Organ at Broadway," *Lexington Herald* (Nov. 10, 1902).

25 "Quits Church," *Lexington Leader* (Nov. 3, 1902).

26 "Organ Voted Into Broadway Church," *Lexington Herald* (Nov. 24, 1902).

27 As the *Lexington Leader* reported: "The result of this balloting was in no sense a surprise, it being pretty well settled beforehand that the proposition would carry, as there had been a growing sentiment in favor of the organ for the past ten or fifteen years." ("Organ Side Wins," Nov. 24, 1902).

28 "Organ Voted Into Broadway."

29 "Organ Voted Into Broadway" and "Organ Side Wins."

30 "Organ Voted Into Broadway."

31 *Autobiography* 65.

32 "Organ Strains Heard for the First Time in Broadway Church," *Lexington Leader* (Feb. 2, 1903).

33 Douglas W. Carter, *The Origin and Early History of Broadway Christian Church* (Master's Thesis at Cincinnati Bible Seminary, 1992) 97.

President McGarvey
Tells Why He Opposes
the Organ

T he following statement signed by President J.W. McGarvey, of
the Bible College, is self-explanatory:

In justice to myself, and in deference to the wishes of many
friends who know not my reasons for standing against
the use of instrumental music in the public worship of the
church, I hereby, with the editor's kind permission, make
them public. I do this, not for the purpose of provoking controversy, but to show that I am not governed, as some may
suspect, by a blind and unreasoning prejudice. I propose
to be brief, and to this end I shall present only those considerations which seem to me to have the greatest weight:

First – The acts of public worship in the church of God are
matters of divine appointment, and not of human choice.
Men could not know what acts in the way of worship would
be acceptable to God but for a revelation of His will on
the subject. With respect to Christian worship as distinguished from the Jewish, we are to find this revelation in
the teaching of Christ and his apostles. In this teaching we

find express authority for singing, but none for instrumental music. It is an acknowledged fact that the latter music was never used in churches planted by the apostles and their fellow-laborers. This apostolic precedent had such force with subsequent generations of Christians, that no instrument was used in any church for a period of more than seven hundred years. This first, of which we have an historical account, was an organ placed in the church at Aix-la-Chapelle, by the Emperor Charlemagne in the year 757. Its use was for a long time violently opposed by monks and clergy of the Roman Catholic Church, but the innovation gradually won its way, and after a struggle of nearly eight hundred years it was at last officially recognized by the Council of Trent which convened in 1545. (Schaff-Herzog Cyclopedia, Art. Organ, Prof. Hauck).

Second – This omission of instrumental music from Christian worship has greater significance from the fact that in Jewish worship it had been in use from the time of David and continued to be until the destruction of Jerusalem by the Romans. The apostles who instituted the former worship had been accustomed to its use in the latter, and it was known to have had the divine approval expressed by inspired prophets. When, therefore, under the control of the Holy Spirit within them they deliberately omitted from the new form of worship this element of the old, the divine will that it should be continued no longer was as plain as day. It was laid aside, as was the burning of incense, the purifications from legal uncleanness and other elements of the Jewish ritual, all of which were included in what Paul styles "the bond written in ordinances" which Christ "blotted out," "nailing it to his cross" (Col. 2:14 [ASV]). Nothing short of this decisive work of the Holy Spirit could have prevented the Jewish Christians from using the accustomed instruments, or could have kept their use out of the church for seven centuries. I feel that I cannot be mistaken about this indication of the divine will.

Third – From the fact stated above that acts of worship are matters of divine appointment and not of human choice, it follows that all such acts not authorized by the scriptures are acts of will-worship; and all will-worship is expressly condemned by the apostle Paul. Speaking of certain ordinances which were after the precepts and doctrines of men, he says, "Which things have indeed a show of wisdom in will-worship, and humility, and severity to the body; but are not of any value against the indulgence of the flesh." (Col. 2:20-23 [ASV]). Jesus also rebuked Pharisees for adding to the ordinances of the law, saying, in the words of Isaiah, who gave the same rebuke to his contemporaries: "in vain do they worship me, Teaching as their doctrines the precepts of men."(Matt. 15:9 [ASV]).

These three are my principal reasons for the position which I occupy. I have others, but I will not take the space to give them. [Lest], however I should appear, to those unacquainted with the history of the subject, to be occupying a position peculiar to myself, I call attention to some historical facts. While this innovation forced its way by a long struggle into the Roman Catholic Church, the Greek Church, which includes many millions of adherents, has always rejected it, and vocal music alone is used in its assemblies to this day. The same is true of the Armenian Church, and these two bodies date from the time of the apostles. Again, while the Church of Rome brought the organ with them, the other Protestant bodies, such as Presbyterians, the Baptists and the Methodists, started on their career without it, and it was not until the nineteenth century, and chiefly during the middle part of it, that the innovation gradually crept into these churches. It was resisted with great earnestness by strong men, notably by such eminent theologians as Dr. R.J. Breckinridge, of whose determined opposition till the day of his death the readers of *The Morning Herald* saw an elegant account in that paper on Sunday last (November 9). I remember very distinctly the debates on the subject that agitated the Presbyterian Church fifty years ago, and I learned much from the debatants.

It was not until the year 1869, so far as I know, that an organ was used in a church of the Disciples. It caused a schism in the church. This was in St. Louis. A committee of eminent brethren, including with others, President Graham and Isaac Errett, was called to settle the controversy, and they did so by deciding that the organ should be set aside, and that the separated members should then return to the church. Since then the innovation has rapidly gained headway among us as it did in other religious bodies. In common with F.G. Allen of this State, and other eminent men in other States, I contended against it until we were overborne by "the spirit of the age."

I conclude by stating that notwithstanding by serious convictions on the subject, I would, under protest, retain my membership in a church which uses the organ, rather than be cut off from the other ordinances of the Lord's house; but that so long as I can choose between such a church and one that worships without it, I cannot hesitate what to do.

With ill will toward no human being, and with a most earnest desire for peace in my old age, I here leave the subject.

–J.W. McGarvey

To Vote Next Sunday

The vote on the organ will be taken at the Broadway Church next Sunday. Following is a copy of the resolution defeated at the meeting last Sunday:

Whereas, Some devout and earnest Christian men and women

of this congregation are opposed to the use of the organ in worship, some of them from a preference for other music, some from a conviction that the use of the organ in worship is not scriptural, and others because they believe the organ is not worth the price we are about to pay for its introduction, and,

Whereas, Our beloved Elder, J.W. McGarvey, has notified us that for conscience's sake he must withdraw from this congregation if the organ is introduced into our worship, and,

Whereas, He has faithfully devoted a long and useful life to the service of the Christian Church at large as editor, teacher, preacher and counselor, winning by his labors both national and international reputation for a knowledge of the Bible such as few men have attained among our people, so that his name is known and honored by disciples from the Atlantic to the Pacific, in the islands of the sea and wherever our plea has gone, and,

Whereas, By his services to this congregation as one of its founders, as its teacher and preacher for many years, and as an elder of this day, he has placed us under an especial debt of gratitude, such that the kindest and loving ministrations can never repay, even though they be fondly showered upon him for all the rest of his life – a life now passing into a gentle, loving, and beautiful old age – therefore, be it

Resolved, By this congregation that the consideration of the introduction of the organ into our worship be indefinitely postponed.

The Contest

On this resolution is based the contest which developed last Sunday, and which led to the postponement of the vote on the organ until next Sunday, that a greater number of the congregation might be present. Many of the members have long favored the institution of an organ, but Elder McGarvey's attitude discouraged any expression of their choice, until recently. The withdrawal of President McGarvey when the elders decided to submit the question to a vote several Sundays ago led to the present contest. Each faction is determined and believes it is right, and the outcome will have important bearing on the future of the church. ❏

Quoted from "Prest. M'Garvey Tells Why He Opposes Organ," Lexington Herald, *Nov. 16, 1902.*

Why Restoration Still Matters
by Brandon Renfroe

Two hundred years ago, a movement was launched that changed the religious landscape of America. Unlike the leading figures of Protestantism who sought to curb the excesses of a corrupted "Christendom," these pioneers had a different purpose. Believing that the New Testament furnishes the pattern for "all things that pertain unto life and godliness" (2 Peter 1:3), they sought a complete return to the practice of primitive Christianity. We stand today as heirs of this rich legacy.

Conflicting Perspectives

How to understand this heritage best is warmly debated. The "elitists" among us view the Restoration mindset as an antiquated approach to the Scriptures or the unfortunate but perhaps inevitable brainchild of men who labored under the influence of English philosophers. If the Restoration Movement has any modern relevance to these liberal thinkers, it is restricted to a vague plea for unity, which amounts to ecumenism – the recognition of virtually all religious bodies as "Christian," however slight their affiliation with the Savior.

Even those who embrace the ideals of the Restoration are divided as to how its tenets are to be applied. Some contend that the movement is free to evolve, changing as custom or circumstance might dictate. Believing that truth is relative, their attitude is fairly summarized in the words of Friedrich Nietzsche: "There are no facts, only interpretations." Others insist that although culture is fluid, biblical precepts are static – as unchanging as the God who gave them (cf. Malachi 3:6).

In truth, these conflicting viewpoints are nearly as old as the Restoration Movement itself. During its second generation, the "change agent" movement was already in embryonic form as pseudo-progressives sought to reconfigure the church.

In an essay that would prove to be a watershed moment, A.S. Hayden argued:

> Our work is the same as that of the venerable Thomas Campbell, the cherished Alexander Campbell, the valiant Walter Scott, the beloved B.W. Stone, and others; – the recovery of primitive Christianity from the rubbish of the ages and its re-implantation in society in this 19th century. But even since those masters began their work, an entire age and more of human years has gone slowly down the abyss of time, and we are now in a new age, a new world. That old world died with the agents and actors, great and good, who adapted themselves to that then living age, and filled it with their works and their spirit. But that age is not our present living world. We must live in this present active world, not in the world which died with our fathers. [1]

Hayden portrayed any who would dispute with him as opponents of progress: "Progression! Are we alarmed at the word! While all things about us are moving forward, shall we be motionless?" [2] In penning the biography of J.W. McGarvey, W.C. Morro (a former McGarvey pupil) echoed Hayden's sentiments:

> The viewpoint and the motive in studying the Bible today differ from those of McGarvey's time. Hence this age can profit from McGarvey, not by literally doing and teaching as he did, but by meeting the problems that confront it in the spirit and with the ideals of McGarvey. ... So may the Disciples of the mid-twentieth century follow in the steps

of McGarvey and others of his day. Other ways of imitating
the past with profit there are not. [3]

Like Hayden, Morro paid a backhanded homage to the legacy of the
pioneers, believing all that was necessary to follow in their steps was
a loose – and never carefully defined – kinship in "spirit." It is clear
what "Be silent where the Bible is silent" meant to these brethren – the
license to engage in practices not explicitly condemned by Scripture.

Morro would have honored the memory of McGarvey and rendered
the cause of truth a valuable service had he printed his teacher's blunt
reaction to Hayden's essay: "[T]he progress which Bro. Hayden's article
is intended peculiarly to advance, finds in me an enemy." [4] If nothing
else, the exchange indicated that battle lines were quickly being drawn
with the future direction of the movement at stake.

The Value of Restoration

To the chagrin of those who cherish it, an increasing number of Christians have precious little knowledge of the Restoration Movement. Others
view it with a passing curiosity before relegating it mentally to the museum
of "ancient history." Regrettably, many who are interested often obtain
their information from questionable sources (i.e., those who misrepresent
the pioneers to further their own theological agendas). Is there any wonder we slowly are being "destroyed for lack of knowledge"(Hosea 4:6)?

The true value of history is its ability to place the present in a proper
context. So we should learn to appreciate Restoration history as a living,
vibrant and powerful force. But *why* does the movement still matter
in the 21st century?

• **Because of the nature of the church.** If the church is a denomi-
national body, the very premise of restoration is rendered moot. Unlike modern liberalists, the pioneers believed in the uniqueness of the
church of Christ. Although wide enough to include the world, they
knew the church was in fact composed only of those who had been
"born again" according to the precise teaching of the New Testament
(cf. John 3:3-5). Further, they believed those saved from their past sins
should worship as directed by the Word of God. Far from rejecting
any notion of "patternism," the pioneers recognized a divine standard
to which men must conform.

• **Because of the importance of unity.** In the shadow of the cross, Christ prayed for unity among His followers (John 17:20-21). This single-mindedness on the part of His disciples would demonstrate to an unbelieving world the reality of the Savior's claim to be the Son of God. This unity is not to derive from an amalgamated confederation of religionists, united in theory but separated in practice by creeds, catechisms and man-made dogmas. Rather, it is to be grounded in a fervent belief in the all-sufficiency of the Scriptures. "Union," David Lipscomb contended, "is possible only in Christ. Union outside of Christ is union against Christ." [5]

• **Because of the tendency for man to drift.** Moses had barely ascended Mount Sinai before the Israelites, eyewitnesses to astounding miracles of deliverance, reverted to the most blatant idolatry imaginable. A few years removed from the death of Joshua was the rise of a generation "who did not know the Lord" (Judges 2:10). In the first century, Paul chastised the Galatians for "turning away so soon" from the first principles of the gospel (Galatians 1:6). As long as men are weak and sinful, there will be a need for restoration.

• **Because our decisions have consequences.** Although he argued for Universalism, the conscience of Scottish commentator William Barclay seemed repulsed by the notion. "It cannot reasonably be held," he claimed, "that the end of the good man and the end of the bad man are one and the same." [6] Barclay recognized intuitively that for life to have meaning, our decisions must have consequences.

In similar fashion, we must decide which model of restoration we will embrace: that advocated by progressives, in which truth is in a constant state of flux, or that championed by the Bible itself, which calls upon men to seek "the old paths, where [is] the good way" (Jeremiah 6:16). Can divergent spiritual pathways lead to identical eternal destinies? Another thought for the "enlightened" to contemplate: Does a survey of sacred history suggest that "innovators" tend to gravitate toward the truth or migrate away from it? What lessons does Jeroboam teach us (cf. 1 Kings 14:16)?

It may be that some never acquire a taste for Restoration studies. Such is not necessary; one may enter heaven blissfully unaware of the happenings at Cane Ridge. If we fail to interest others in Campbell,

Stone or Scott, we can still have a deep and abiding love for the principles for which they pleaded. May we all learn that God is searching, not for those who presume to instruct Him, but for poor and contrite souls who tremble at His Word (Isaiah 66:2). ❏

Reprinted with permission Gospel Advocate *magazine, March 2011, pp 22-23.*

Endnotes

1 *Millennial Harbinger* (March 1868) 139-140.

2 *Harbinger* (March 1868) 144.

3 W.C. Morro, *Brother McGarvey* (St. Louis: Bethany Press, 1940) 250.

4 *Harbinger* (April 1868) 214.

5 Robert Hooper, *Crying in the Wilderness* (Nashville: McQuiddy Printing, 1979) 299.

6 William Barclay, *Commentary on Matthew*, vol. 1 (Philadelphia: Westminster Press, 1975) 180.

Alphabetical Index of Sermons